BFI Film Classics

The BFI Film Classics series introduces, interprets and celebrates landmarks of world cinema. Each volume offers an argument for the film's 'classic' status, together with discussion of its production and reception history, its place within a genre or national cinema, an account of its technical and aesthetic importance, and in many cases, the author's personal response to the film.

For a full list of titles in the series, please visit
https://www.bloomsbury.com/uk/series/bfi-film-classics/

Point Blank

Eric G. Wilson

THE BRITISH FILM INSTITUTE
Bloomsbury Publishing Plc
50 Bedford Square, London, WC1B 3DP, UK
1385 Broadway, New York, NY 10018, USA
29 Earlsfort Terrace, Dublin 2, Ireland

BLOOMSBURY is a trademark of Bloomsbury Publishing Plc

First published in Great Britain 2023 by Bloomsbury on behalf of the
British Film Institute
21 Stephen Street, London W1T 1LN
www.bfi.org.uk

The BFI is the lead organisation for film in the UK and the distributor of Lottery funds for film.
Our mission is to ensure that film is central to our cultural life, in particular by supporting and
nurturing the next generation of filmmakers and audiences. We serve a public role which covers
the cultural, creative and economic aspects of film in the UK.

Cover artwork: © Nick Morley, linocutboy.com
Series cover design: Louise Dugdale
Series text design: Ketchup/SE14
Images from *Point Blank* (John Boorman, 1967), © Metro-Goldwyn-Mayer; *Catch Us If You Can* (John
Boorman, 1965), © Warner Bros. Pictures Inc./Anglo Amalgamated Distributors Ltd; *Hiroshima mon
amour* (Alan Resnais, 1959), Argos Films/Como Films/Daiei Motion Picture Co. Ltd/Pathe Overseas
Productions; *The Killers* (Donald Siegel, 1964), © Revue Productions; *Rio Bravo* (Howard Hawks,
1958), © Armada Productions Inc. Film stills courtesy BFI National Archive

A catalogue record for this book is available from the British Library.

A catalog record for this book is available from the Library of Congress.

ISBN: PB: 978-1-8390-2576-1
         ePDF: 978-1-8390-2573-0
         ePUB: 978-1-8390-2575-4

Produced for Bloomsbury Publishing Plc by Sophie Contento
Printed and bound in India

To find out more about our authors and books visit www.bloomsbury.com
and sign up for our newsletters.

Contents

Acknowledgments 6

1 The Grail 7

2 Minimalism 11

3 Stoic and Clown 22

4 Los Angeles 29

5 What It Is, Is What You See 37

6 Space and Time 42

7 The Movie House 54

8 Golden Androgyny 59

9 Ironic Genre 71

10 Neurotic Inertia 75

11 Dissolution 84

12 Sex and Sadism 94

Notes 102

Credits 108

Bibliography 110

Acknowledgments

I would like to thank the librarians at the Lilly Library at Indiana University in Bloomington, Indiana. With expertise and good cheer, they helped me navigate the extensive Boorman archive housed in the library and permitted me to cite materials in this book. I would also like to thank the librarians in the British Film Institute's National Archive, who generously assisted my study of MSS and stills related to *Point Blank*. Rebecca Barden, my editor at Bloomsbury, was a great pleasure to work with, as was her assistant editor, Veidehi Hans, and the project manager, Sophie Contento. I am grateful to Jessica Richards, my chair at Wake Forest University, for supporting my proposals for funding to conduct research in London; and I am thankful to Wake Forest for its financial support. Conversations with John McElwee, Philip Arnold and Angus MacLachlan were essential to this book. But nothing would have happened without the generous, intelligent influence of my wife Fielding King.

1 The Grail

An ominous beginning

Lee Marvin squints into lurid red light. This is the first image of John Boorman's *Point Blank* (1967). Where is Marvin? We don't know. But we see that he isn't the sardonically insouciant colonel of *The Dirty Dozen* (1967) or the arrogant heavy of *The Big Heat* (1953). This man is baffled, vulnerable.

Two gunshots explode and Marvin stumbles backwards into the corner of a small concrete room. He lands on a cot. This is a prison cell, and Marvin's fingers twitch. Death spasms. Then Marvin in voiceover: 'Cell ... prison cell. How did I get here?'

Another cut, to a room teeming with sweaty men in black suits. A party. They are drunk. A man plays a plaintive harmonica.

This is the fragmentation of nightmare. Such violence towards space and time intensifies as the film rolls, as does violence towards people. And objects. When Marvin isn't roughing up men or contorting his present back into his traumatic past, he is firing his .44 Magnum into a bed or crashing a convertible into a concrete pillar.

But the film's emotional aggression disturbs far more than the physical. As Marvin's character seeks retribution from the man who shot him in the prison cell – his best friend – and the woman who abetted the man – his wife – he is tortured by betrayal, loss and loneliness.

If *Point Blank* on the surface is a simple revenge thriller, an eye for an eye, its core is spiritual, intricate, a yearning to heal a broken soul. The picture's rupturing of continuity mirrors trauma's demonic flashbacks, while its rare moments of spontaneous affection proffer redemption, release into an ecstatic *now*.

Point Blank's melding of fractured psychomachia and revenge saga makes it virtually unique among Hollywood thrillers. Disorienting hybridity also characterises the film's style, a compound of neo-noir and nouvelle vague. The movie's ideas of gender are unexpected, too, especially from a work that has been compared to *High Plains Drifter* (1973) and *Death Wish* (1974), fables of ruthlessly masculine retaliation. In *Point Blank*, traditional markers of male strength – like combativeness and rationality – are weaknesses, whereas qualities usually associated with the feminine, such as patience and emotion, invigorate. Another remarkable element of *Point Blank*, packaged as a tight-jawed sortie into sex and sadism, is its comedy. Boorman often exaggerates conventional Hollywood violence to the point of absurdist humour.

* * *

Boorman first explored the main theme of *Point Blank* – the quest for wholeness – in his initial foray into dramatic cinema. (Heretofore he was a documentarian.) In 1964, he made for the BBC, then his employer, a film called *The Quarry*, about a sculptor named Arthur King. He is a modern incarnation of the mythical monarch, and he attempts to chisel a large block of stone into his personal Grail.

The Quarry caught the attention of producer David Deutsch. Deutsch had just released Clive Donner's clever black comedy *Nothing But the Best* (1964), starring Alan Bates and shot by

Nicolas Roeg, and he was looking for other young talent. He asked Boorman what sort of movie he'd like to make. Still captivated by King Arthur, Boorman suggested a story based on John Cowper Powys's *A Glastonbury Romance* (1932), a novel that imagines the Grail legend in a modern setting. Deutsch found this idea ponderous, and he convinced Boorman to direct a pop music rollick that would capitalise on the Beatles' very successful *A Hard Day's Night* (1964). Standing in for the Fab Four would be The Dave Clark Five. The film had already been sold to Warner Bros., who assumed that profit, by virtue of the band's popularity, was guaranteed.[1]

Boorman muted the Beatles' exuberance. Where the Beatles comically flee adoring fans as they travel from Liverpool to London, Dave Clark, as Steve the Stuntman, bitterly abandons the UK's capital to escape its commercialism. Dinah (Barbara Ferris), an attractive young model who is the face of a meat industry advertising campaign ('Meat for Go'), joins Steve. (The other members of Clark's band, also stuntmen in the movie, play minor roles.) Steve and Dinah's quest is picaresque, and it begins winningly enough, with a London slapstick sequence reminiscent of Richard Lester's staccato editing in *A Hard Day's Night*. But after Steve and Dinah leave for Burgh, an island off the coast of Devon, the pace slows. In scene after scene, reality undermines the couple's idealism. When they reach the island, they find it's not off the grid at all. You can walk to it from the mainland when the tide is out. Waiting in a deserted resort is Leon Zissell (David de Keyser), the executive who masterminded the advertising campaign. Defeated, Dinah returns to her role as Zissell's model, while Steve heads out with the boys to scuba dive in Spain.

In depicting a quest for a utopia, Boorman filmed his Grail movie anyway, even if the failed adventure in *Catch Us If You Can* (1965) is more a parody of Arthurian lore than a celebration. In several subsequent films – including *Point Blank*, *Deliverance* (1972), *Zardoz* (1974) and *Excalibur* (1981) – Boorman likewise darkens Arcadian visions. For his heroes, even King Arthur, there is no elixir

Catch Us If You Can (1965): no utopia

that can fully heal the pains of life. Boorman's quests are ironic. They raise hopes of redemption only to blight them.

Despite the sadness of *Catch Us If You Can* – especially for the kind of film where the boy usually gets the girl – critics in the UK and US (where the picture was retitled *Having a Wild Weekend*) were more-or-less kind to the movie. It was in fact the film's pessimism that garnered its most important review, from the formidable Pauline Kael, who valued the movie's 'connotations of sadness, of nostalgia, and perhaps of something one might call truth. It is one of those films that linger in the memory.'[2]

Even though Kael also found the picture's tone 'uneven' and its style 'faltering',[3] her analysis of Boorman's first big-studio movie – like a golden ticket from Wonka – gave the young British director, in his own words, 'a degree of credibility in Hollywood'.[4] Within months he found himself sitting across from the world's biggest movie star.

2 Minimalism

Just after completing his DC5 picture, however, Boorman had no thought of Hollywood. He planned to return to the BBC, where he would make documentaries on D. W. Griffith and Christopher Isherwood, men integral to his understanding of cinema.

To undertake these projects, Boorman flew to the US in 1965. He marvelled at Griffith's desire to 'photograph the wind on the wheat'. He stared in 'lonely wonder' at LA's 'flimsy facades, the absence of architecture, its shapes defined only by neon signs and vast hoardings, tangles of power cables looping across the sky'. He met Elvis; the King's 'handshake was so limp that his hand felt boneless'.[5]

While in LA, Boorman met with MGM producers Bob Chartoff, Irwin Winkler and Judd Bernard. The Kael review had led to Boorman being noticed, and big studios were keen just then on European directors who shot stylistically bold films on modest budgets. The producers invited Boorman to pitch. He proposed his Glastonbury project but once again elicited no interest. Well, then, what about a 'modern noir thriller?' The producers perked up. Nothing definite came from the meeting, though. Boorman returned to London to edit his Griffith documentary.[6]

Bernard showed up in the city soon after and presented Boorman a script based on a Donald E. Westlake (aka Richard Stark) novel called *The Hunter* (1962). It was by Rafe and David Newhouse and told of the revenge quest of one Parker, Westlake's protagonist. Boorman found it terrible. Bernard had also passed the script to Lee Marvin, then in London filming *The Dirty Dozen*, his follow-up to *Cat Ballou* (1965), which had won him an Academy Award, and *The Professionals* (1966), his first cinematic foray into the role that would make him most famous: the Hemingwayesque anti-hero, world-weary and cynical, yet highly skilled in his dangerous work (he is a mercenary) and gifted with a biting sense of humour. (Marvin initially developed this character on TV, in *M Squad* [NBC, 1957–60], in which he played Frank Ballinger, a take-no-shit Chicago cop with a sensitive side.)

Bernard arranged for Boorman to meet Marvin at an Italian restaurant in Soho. The producer would join them. Boorman was nervous. Coming off his Oscar, Marvin was a colossal movie star, and he had a reputation for drunken brashness. And then there was his physical presence: he was a muscular 6'2"; his head was epically large, evoking an Easter Island bust, and it was capped with prematurely white hair; his blue eyes were icicle shards; and his baritone voice boomed imperiously. (His big, soft lips suggested vulnerability, though, and maybe there was a hint of sadness in his speech.) When Boorman came face-to-face with the actor, he observed that 'everything around seemed diminished – the tables and chairs were too small, the waiters dwarfed. I felt like a miniature creature from another, tinier planet.'[7]

The meeting did not go well. Marvin, who spurned chit-chat, immediately asked Boorman what he thought of the script. The director was honest: one cliché after another. Marvin agreed. So why, the actor wondered, are we even here?

I am interested in the main character, Boorman ventured. Parker. (Or, as he would be called in the movie, Walker.) He is double-crossed by his wife and his best friend, and his quest for revenge is futile. As Boorman described the betrayal, a memory flooded his consciousness: how his own mother had had an affair with a man named Herbert, and his father had known about it. Boorman suspects that Marvin sensed the disturbance, perhaps catching an 'emotional resonance in my voice'.[8] The actor said little and left right after eating.

Bernard was furious. He had placed Boorman across the table from a world-class star, and he had blown it. Never knock the material! Always talk about how great the rewrite will be. The producer pestered Boorman to take another run at Marvin.

That Marvin agreed to meet and even invited the director to his flat suggests that the seasoned actor saw something in the younger man – an intelligence and an emotional depth. But Marvin, like Boorman, was also intrigued by the script's protagonist.

Boorman elaborated on his earlier description of the character:

I suggested that Walker had been emotionally and physically wounded to a point where he was no longer human. This made him frightening, but also pure, in a certain sense. He was beyond vanity and desire. His only connection with life was through violence, yet he lacked the conviction or cruelty or passion to take pleasure from it, or satisfaction from vengeance.[9]

Why would Marvin, who specialised in portraying caustic baddies and stoic gunmen, be drawn to such a character? During several more meetings with Boorman throughout the summer and autumn of 1966, Marvin revealed that he saw himself in Westlake's character. Like Walker, Marvin had been traumatised. He had served as a Marine in the Pacific Theatre during World War II. On 18 June 1944, Marvin's unit was ordered to take Mount Tapochau on the island of Saipan. As a scout sniper, Marvin was one of the first to begin the ascent of the 1,500-foot peak. The enemy spotted him and opened fire. Marvin was hit in the sciatic nerve, just below his spine. Another bullet caught his foot. The battle was a massacre. Marvin was one of only six out of 247 who survived.[10]

Marvin recounted other wartime memories. He had killed, taking out Japanese soldiers at night from a rubber boat floating near their shores. He had been afraid. And he felt guilty. Why had he survived when so many others had died?[11]

Marvin feared 'he had lost some essential element of his humanity'.[12] He saw the same terror in Walker. The character's hunger for revenge against his best friend and his wife was more than a crime genre trope. It was a quest to recover his lost Grail: his ability to love, laugh, play. Marvin believed that in portraying Walker he could work through his own trauma.

One autumn night, after a long session of drinking, Marvin looked at Boorman, paused, and then announced that he would do the film. But only on one condition: the script goes. And Marvin tossed it out of the window. 'It floated down two stories, opening out, the pages fluttering like wings, until it came to rest in the gutter, a dying bird.'[13]

After working with Marvin on the film, Boorman would come to see this 'defining gesture' as indicative of the performer's skill in finding the 'perfect cinematic metaphor'.[14]

(Boorman is fond of a little joke that arose from this moment. Soon after the release of *Payback* [1999], a Mel Gibson vehicle also based on *The Hunter*, Boorman was asked his opinion of the picture. He said he had not seen it, but he had read the script. It was uncannily similar to the one Marvin had thrown out of the window over thirty years earlier. Did a very young Mel pass by as the papers fluttered down, and did he gather them from the gutter and later turn them into a bad movie?[15])

* * *

On the strength of Marvin's promise to do the film, Boorman left the BBC in November of 1966 and moved to LA. He installed himself in the Hotel Bel-Air, along with his wife and four children, and he and Alex Jacobs, an old BBC friend and colleague, worked on the script. Meanwhile, MGM set the film's budget at $2 million.

Boorman and Jacobs found the Newhouse script unusable. The brothers had turned Westlake's elliptical, deadpan, brutal novel into 'a somewhat dated and slightly nostalgic gangster story in the style of Raymond Chandler'.[16] Boorman and Jacobs wanted to create a more 'enterprising' thriller. Jacobs believed that television had fatigued Hollywood conventions. A vibrant film would need to be unpredictable, 'half a reel ahead of the audience'. Speed was essential, cutting abruptly from one essential scene to the next, with 'no people getting in and out of cars, no shots of car doors opening and closing'.[17] Integral to this quickness, Boorman thought, was minimal dialogue. Too much talk had plagued even the best traditional thrillers, like Howard Hawks's *The Big Sleep* (1946).[18]

Westlake's novel featured both a fractured narrative and terse dialogue. Boorman and Jacobs didn't look to the novel for inspiration, however. Their formal and verbal choices were guided by Alain Resnais and Harold Pinter.[19]

Resnais' *Hiroshima mon amour* (1959) contemplates trauma and time. The film opens with a close-up of the torsos and arms of two bodies intertwined, as if in an erotic embrace. Ash falls on the flesh. The shot evokes the ashes falling on bodies in the aftermath

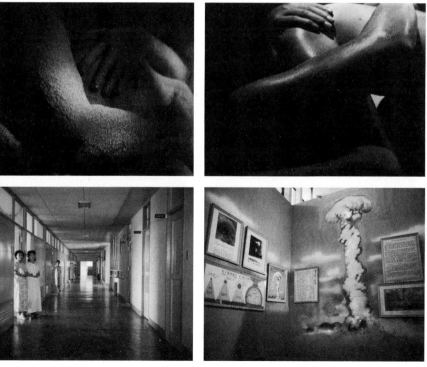

Hiroshima mon amour (1959): bodies covered in atomic ash; erotic bodies; the wounded; the museum

of the Hiroshima bombing. The lack of context, however, and the absence of faces suggest dream. A dissolve, and the bodies are clean of ash. They have now changed positions, and the scene is definitively sexual. Another dissolve, and the flesh is sweaty. Then a man's voiceover, saying, 'You saw nothing in Hiroshima. Nothing.' A woman in voiceover replies, 'I saw the hospital', and the camera cuts to the wounded in a hospital, and then back to the bodies, and once more the man says the woman has seen nothing of Hiroshima, and she says that she has been to the museum in Hiroshima four times, and the film shifts to a museum commemorating the tragedy. Are these scenes the woman's memories? The man says they aren't. The woman insists they are.

Trauma shatters the boundary between past and present. So intense is the pain, that the sufferer can't stop thinking about it, and so the past is just as real as the present, sometimes indistinguishable from it. But if the present is the past, is the present really occurring? Has the past, passed?

A film about a tortured character who confuses past and present, *Point Blank* also disorients time (as well as space). But Boorman's movie doesn't only fracture its images; it also fragments its speech, inspired by the minimalist brilliance of Pinter. In plays like *The Homecoming* (1965) and scripts like *The Servant* (1963), Pinter's terse dialogue and awkward pauses hint at a barely repressed menace. Brothers insinuate resentment while talking about a cheese roll. A couple invites suspicion in discussing where a vase of flowers should go. It's what's not said that resonates most powerfully. This ominous indirection characterises Marvin's speech in *Point Blank*: his character's trauma is too deep for words, so he sits in awkward silence or grimly repeats the same clipped questions.

As Boorman and Jacobs worked on the script during the winter of 1966 and the spring of 1967, they stripped the story to its barest essentials. At the same time, they strengthened the depth of the characters. They turned the Rose character of the novel – a walk-on prostitute who helps Walker find his betrayer – into the sister of Walker's unfaithful wife. Boorman and Jacobs imagined this character – called Chris in the film – as Walker's love interest. She alone draws out Walker's softer side. In his unpublished notes from the earliest stages of script development, Boorman imagines a moment, very tender, when Chris makes Walker laugh. The response is so difficult for the hardened Walker that it comes awkwardly, like a kid trying to ride a bike for the first time. Right after this interchange, Walker feels remorse for his surly treatment of Chris, and he wants to apologise, but doesn't know how.[20]

While adding nuance, Boorman and Jacobs cut exposition. Boorman initially saw Walker escaping from Alcatraz in a dinghy. In the film, however, his means of escape remains mysterious. Boorman early on also had Walker stalking his wife – her name is Lynne – before confronting her about her betrayal. This sequence would unfold over several days and establish Lynne's promiscuity.[21] But in the movie, almost immediately after Walker discovers Lynne's whereabouts, he bursts through her door.

These decisions demonstrate Boorman's, and Jacobs's, commitment to the idea that an emotional life isn't causal and continuous (*if* this action occurs, *then* this result clearly follows). It is illogical, perplexing. Walker survives his seemingly fatal wound at Alcatraz because he survives his wound at Alcatraz. And why demonstrate Lynne's sexual habits? She betrayed Walker. That is what happened.

The same logic applies to Lynne's flashback of her first meeting with Walker. In the beginning, Boorman imagined Walker flirtatiously circling her on a motorcycle.[22] In the film, though, Walker finds his future wife while walking along a dock; the two face one another and begin to move, impishly, in a circle. Boorman rejects a clichéd symbol of male virility, a motorcycle, and depicts a strange, accidental dance.

According to Jacobs, a first draft of the script was completed during his visit to the US in the early winter of 1966, and a second produced once he was back in the UK, inspired by letters and phone calls between him and Boorman. In the first of these letters, from

Jacobs to Boorman, dated 19 December 1966, Jacobs argues that
Walker's character needs still more complexity. He should appear as
a man torn between rectitude and tenderness, and audiences should
understand that it is this conflict that incites his extreme violence.[23]

Jacobs also thinks Walker should be responsible for Lynne's
betrayal. She is intimidated by Walker's intensity, and she drifts to his
best friend, named Mal, whose crudeness arouses her promiscuity.[24]

The second draft was completed by the time filming began on
20 February 1967. Jacobs returned to the US to be on set for the
first two weeks. There he made further revisions, particularly to the
ending. He was still making changes when he returned to the UK in
March. He wrote to Boorman that his main concern had not yet been
resolved: the relationship between Walker and Chris. He imagines a
penultimate scene in which a member of a crime syndicate, called the
Organisation, taunts Walker. Walker erupts into a terrific fury. Chris
is present. She and Walker had made love the night before. Only
she can calm him, by reminding him of his abiding virtues. Once he
affirms Chris's appreciation of his character, he is ready for a final
showdown with his enemy.[25]

This ending would be operatic. Once Walker finds out that the
boss of the Organisation has been manipulating him all along, he
savagely advances on the man. The man fires three shots. He misses.
He suddenly feels old and weak, and he stumbles off a parapet to his
death. Chris leads an addled Walker towards a brighter future. This
melodramatic moment would be justified, Jacobs thought, if it were
made clear the night before that the two are in love.[26]

Boorman didn't shoot the conclusion Jacobs envisioned, nor the
love scene. This decision troubled Jacobs, who felt that the finished
film was too cold.[27] In the final draft of the screenplay, Boorman
minimised the romance between Chris and Walker, and his ending is
non-violent and haunting.

Like Walter Hill several years later, Boorman valued Jacobs
for his haiku-like brevity, capable of revealing potent subtleties that
more thorough pronouncements overlook.[28] Ultimately, though,

Boorman found Jacobs a bit on the sentimental side, too traditionally Hollywood: too predictable, continuous and romantic. Boorman saw Walker more realistically, as a man too damaged to fall in love or enjoy redemption. This is not to say that Boorman's Walker has lost all liveliness or compassion. He retains these qualities, but they are dormant. Fearing that he will be betrayed once more, he has buried them. But there are moments, and they are with Chris, when Walker's vitals pulse once more, and when they do, so comatose were they, the effect is powerful and moving, and, strangely enough, *funny*.

* * *

Because Marvin's schedule was so tight, Boorman had to begin shooting while the script was still in development. This compression harried Boorman, but it also allowed him to get Marvin's almost daily feedback as the script was being drafted. Though the most substantial influence on the script was Jacobs – regardless of his somewhat conventional ideas of character – the second most important shaper was Marvin.

Boorman would drive out to Malibu to find Marvin on the terrace of his small beach house, where he lived tumultuously with the actress Michelle Triola. The director would share with his actor the work he and Jacobs had completed earlier that day, and Marvin would press the story closer to wordless action, sinewy metaphor.

Boorman told Marvin about the early scene in which Walker crashes through Lynne's door, gun drawn, hoping to find Mal, his nemesis, in her bed. The bed is empty. Walker fires six bullets into the mattress. Boorman saw this action as a sign of Walker's 'frustration, the emptiness of revenge'.[29] But would the moment come off as risible?

Marvin liked the idea. This was his style of acting – gesture before speech. But he refined the scene. He would wield a very large pistol, a Smith & Wesson .44 Magnum (later of *Dirty Harry* [1971] fame), to emphasise the sad gap between the potency Walker wants and the failure he endures. Marvin also proposed that he exaggerate the recoil from the gun: his revenge slamming back, turning on him.

Futility of revenge

Boorman observed that Marvin's feedback was 'allusive, oblique'. 'He leapt from metaphor to metaphor, and when he was drinking, the leaps got wider. ... [T]here was always wisdom there, deep dark thoughts that touched on our enterprise.'[30]

(Marvin's drinking was notorious. One Saturday morning after an all-nighter, he drove cautiously home down Sunset Blvd. There was his house. When he couldn't find his key, he rang the bell. An unfamiliar woman answered. Marvin had sold this house to her three months earlier. The drunk returned to Sunset. Luckily, someone was selling maps to the homes of the stars. He bought one, but he couldn't find his name. He slept in his car for an hour, woke to find his memory returned, and he made it to his real home.[31])

Marvin influenced the script in rehearsals, too. They took place in his Malibu home. In one scene, just after Walker shoots the bed, he interrogates Lynne (played by Sharon Acker) about Mal's whereabouts. In a rehearsal of the scene, however, Marvin said nothing. Acker reacted by asking Walker's questions herself and then answering them. Boorman found this change beautiful. It signalled that Walker was too depleted to speak, sexually depleted, after emptying his weapon.[32]

Marvin pushed the visual over the verbal on set as well. Just before shooting Walker's reaction to Lynne's death, Marvin encouraged Boorman to imagine the apartment as a manifestation of Walker's torment. He did. After Walker finds his wife dead, he walks back out into the living room and looks out of the window. He returns to the bedroom. But it is empty, except for a bare mattress and a white cat. Where has the body gone? Where are Lynne's things? Walker goes into the living room again. Now it is bare. Walker squats in a corner. The room resembles a prison cell.[33]

Robert O'Brien, president of MGM, thought Boorman's off-script innovations were insane. He called in a psychiatrist. The shrink sat in the corner of O'Brien's office as the boss grilled Boorman on his unorthodox decisions. Boorman couldn't muster a defence. He had made his experiments, he claimed later, 'working at the edge, functioning beyond my limits, open to the instant, in unspoken harmony with the actors, in a state of grace, somewhere between terror and ecstasy'.[34]

In the end the studio had to tolerate Boorman. The director had the star on his side, and O'Brien knew that if he fired Boorman, Marvin would walk. MGM would have to live with the young director, who not only had Marvin's ardent support, but also enjoyed, thanks to Marvin, final cut, extraordinary for such an unproven director.

3 Stoic and Clown

But Marvin and Boorman were not always simpatico. Angie Dickinson, who played Chris, remembers their collaborations as contentious. This memory explains an odd passage in one of Jacobs's letters to Boorman.[35] He refers to Boorman's need to control Marvin. While the actor's instincts are sound, his expression might be problematic. Boorman might use his intellect to manage Marvin's emotions. Also, Jacobs adds, Marvin is vain, and Boorman might use this flaw to his advantage.[36]

But if Marvin's force of personality might have occasionally threatened Boorman, the director generally welcomed his star's intuitions – not only because Marvin was magnificently talented, but also because he possessed a rare bleak wisdom. He knew what it felt like to be dead and live again.

Marvin's ability to stand poised between death and life is his genius. Notice this tension even in his appearance: white hair and frost-blue eyes and puffy wrinkles under them but also the tanned skin of a young man, and a body muscled and lean, and the posture of a dancer. This disconcerting mix of hoariness and vigour forces upon us what Marvin is famous for: calculated ferocity.

But those who knew Marvin best saw in his eyes not just the assassin's inscrutable calm. They also discerned a sadness, a shyness, an abiding sense that the world is a place where terrible things happen, and there's nothing you can do.[37]

What is most vulnerable in Marvin's face, though, are his soft, full lips. But if his mouth is sensitive, almost like a child's, it also expresses Marvin's aptitude, somewhat overlooked, for comedy: his sardonic smirk and his drunken grin. If the former curl of the lip acknowledges the hurt and says, *fuck it*, the latter laughs more uproariously the closer the hangover approaches.

Marvin's Charlie, the crisply professional yet philosophically perplexed hitman in *The Killers* (1964), melds these two comic modes, the understated and the hyperbolic, especially in the final scene, in which he staggers shot and bloody into the suburban home of his nemesis, Jack Browning (played with unintentional hilarity by Ronald Reagan). Though Charlie is in agony, his expression suggests irony: I know it's absurd that I kill for money, but the world is absurd, so why not? But his prolonged, over-the-top lurching is not aloof from the folly. It is farce in full, before he falls like a man of rubber. (Clu Gulager, his co-star, said it was Marvin's drunkenness that relaxed his bones.)

The Killers (1964): ironic hitman

The killing clown

Marvin's insouciant assassin and his agile clown aren't that different. Both master calm in catastrophe. Don Siegel, Marvin's director in *The Killers*, was the first to evoke the actor's detachment amid the turmoil. Boorman was the second. These directors sensed in Marvin what other 'cool' actors of the 1960s, such as Steve McQueen, lacked: a melancholy intelligence beneath the overwrought toughness.

Watch *Point Blank* back-to-back with McQueen's *Bullitt* (1968) to appreciate the difference between Marvin and McQueen. Where Marvin is imposing without trying to be – like an elite athlete, he reserves a playful serenity behind his force – McQueen overplays his indifference – a second-rate competitor straining to transcend his level. Howard Hampton captures this distinction eloquently: Marvin 'projected an air of unhistrionic menace', while McQueen 'was an earnest, unmarked lightweight'. The Clint Eastwood of the 1970s can look even sillier compared to Marvin: he is 'a stick figure caricature, playing at being cool where Marvin embodied an icy intractability all the more persuasive for the shards of pain and doubt and exhaustion you glimpsed around his razor sharp edges'.[38]

* * *

Marvin lent his subtlety to the casting. As one would expect, his and Boorman's choice for the film's second most important character, Chris, clashed with the studio's. According to Irwin Winkler, MGM wanted Stella Stevens for the part. In fact, the studio hired the actress without telling the producer, the director or the star.[39] Stevens was known less for her acting and more for her sex appeal. She had posed for *Playboy* twice, and her film roles, such as Elvis's love interest in *Girls! Girls! Girls!* (1962), had capitalised on her sultriness. For the *Point Blank* that MGM imagined, a sexy crime thriller, Stevens seemed perfect.

For Winkler, she was all wrong. He wanted Angie Dickinson, as did Boorman and Marvin. Once more, Marvin's star power prevailed. He told the studio that if Dickinson were not cast, he would quit.[40]

The casting of Dickinson over Stevens takes us deeper into Boorman's (and Marvin's) vision for *Point Blank*. Marvin had worked with Dickinson in *The Killers*, and so he knew of her talents first-hand. In that film, Dickinson plays the complicated Sheila Farr, at once cynical and sentimental. On the one hand, Sheila is the conniving mistress of aging crook Jack Browning, basically a high-class prostitute willing to do anything for the right price. On the other, she loses her head over young speed freaks like John Cassavetes's Johnny North, and risks alienating her sugar daddy.

Marvin admired Dickinson's talent, not unlike his own, for nuance; she could play cool and vulnerable at the same time. He also had to love her gameness. In one of the most horrifying scenes in *The Killers*, he and his partner dangle a terrified Dickinson out of the window, before Marvin jerks her back inside and slams her into a chair on the other side of the room.

But surely the character Boorman and Marvin had most in mind in casting Dickinson was her Feathers in Howard Hawks's *Rio Bravo* (1958). In that role, Dickinson is the consummate 'Howard Hawks' female. Like Rosalind Russell, Lauren Bacall and Barbara Stanwyck – not to mention Hawks's second wife Nancy 'Slim' Gross – Dickinson is tough and rowdy enough to hang with the boys, and she can match wits with the best of them. But she never loses her sexuality, and she is frank about it, taking the lead in the seduction game, keeping John Wayne's Chance, her crush, on his heels.

Rio Bravo (1958): Feathers keeping the Duke on his heels

It's her subtlety that gives her the edge, her ability to read the signs, as when Chance tells her (jokingly) that he'll arrest her if she wears a skimpy dress in the saloon, and she gets what that really means: he loves her. Her bold behaviour has a price, though; she risks being misunderstood or rejected. Feathers is forthright about this, too – not afraid to express weakness – and it is charming. She kisses Chance, and he doesn't kiss back, and it's clear she's hurt, but she tries again, and he reciprocates, and she has the panache to say, 'It's better when two people do it.'

If Marvin's 'cool' is his stoicism amid chaos, Dickinson's is her confidence despite being exposed. Boorman knew that he needed someone as strong and dexterous as Dickinson to go head-to-head with Marvin. Her Chris cultivates a complex relationship with the saturnine Walker. She simultaneously sympathises with him, fears him, opposes him, mocks him, loves him. Only an actress capable at once of seductiveness, humour, fragility, toughness and generosity could pull off such a role.

It is instructive to pause on other actresses Boorman considered for Chris. In his notes, probably from late winter of 1966, Boorman imagines Chris as either Kim Novak or Joanne Woodward.[41] After her successful run from 1955 to 1960 – which encompassed *The Man with the Golden Arm* (1955), *Vertigo* (1958) and *Strangers When We Meet* (1960) – Novak's career had stalled. Perhaps she would be eager to work, Boorman probably thought, and maybe she could capture the range he wanted for Chris. As *Vertigo* showed, she could move between sexiness and neediness. But could she express both at once? As far as we know, she was never contacted about the part. The same goes for Woodward, though we can certainly see how her expansiveness would have appealed to Boorman. Her Academy Award-winning performance in *The Three Faces of Eve* (1957) featured her playing a mousey southern homemaker, a turbulent sexpot and a sensible, stable young woman.

Boorman initially thought about Dickinson for the Lynne role. Also on his list for Walker's wife were Piper Laurie, Eleanor Parker,

Julie London, Ann Francis, Antoinette Bower, Joanne Woodward
(again) and Sharon Acker. Boorman also jotted down Lee Remick
and Hope Lange in his notes.[42] Acker of course got the part, and
there is no record of MGM contacting these other actresses.

For the Mal role, Boorman contemplated Warren Oates, who
was just finishing up the shooting for *In the Heat of the Night*
(1967).[43] Oates's iconic performance in Monte Hellman's *The
Shooting* (1966) was just behind him, and his equally memorable
role in Sam Peckinpah's *The Wild Bunch* (1969) just ahead. Oates
would not quite have worked for Mal, at least as Boorman eventually
imagined him, because the actor was too magnetic for the role,
always supple and surprising, even when playing average Joes.
Boorman's Mal needs to be the opposite: a lout who nonetheless
believes he is cock of the walk.

Boorman also listed Canadian actor John Vernon, who landed
the role and played it perfectly.[44] In 1966, Vernon was mostly known
for his work in television, especially his crime-fighting coroner
on CBC's *Wojeck* (1966–8). As Vernon showed in *Dirty Harry*
and *Animal House* (1978), he had a gift for playing not-so-smart
men who think they've got it figured. His booming voice initially
impresses but quickly becomes bluster.

Initially, Marvin opposed Vernon's casting. He felt the actor
wasn't 'strong enough' to contend with him. During filming, when
Walker and Mal scuffle, Marvin punched Vernon in the gut, hard
enough to make him cry. Understandably, Vernon protested. His
acting improved after that moment, however; it became angrier,
more intense.[45]

(This is not to excuse Marvin's striking another actor. He
obviously went too far. But this was probably one of the thrills of
working with the man: his garrulousness in a breath could turn
dangerous, and there you were, no longer faking but living.)

After the four leads, the most significant role in the film is that
of Brewster, the Organisation's second in command. Unlike the other
members of the crime syndicate, ruled by corporate seriousness,

Brewster is flamboyant and sarcastic. For him the world is absurd, so why take it seriously? Sure, make a little money and have some fun, but at the end of the day, it's all just a show. When Brewster and Walker face off at the end of the film, the criminal's mockery challenges the protagonist's grim obsession.

Boorman needed an actor who could stand up to Marvin. Carroll O'Connor, on the verge of playing the iconic Archie Bunker in *All in the Family* (CBS, 1971–9), was, perfect. As he would show in this television role and in *Kelly's Heroes* (1970), O'Connor had a talent for boisterous humour. But where these characters are over-the-top without knowing it, O'Connor's Brewster is impishly aware of his hyperbole, and Walker is taken aback, and it's all very funny.

4 Los Angeles

Boorman and Jacobs drafted the story to be set in San Francisco. The night before Boorman was to travel up from LA to check the city out, he ran into Edward G. Robinson, who said, 'You'll love it. It looks like it was built by a drugged-up art collector.'[46]

But Boorman hated the Golden Gate City. 'The gentle hills, the clapboard Victorian villas in pastel colours – it was all utterly wrong for the bleak, cold picture I had in mind.' But LA was just right. Its 'empty arid spaces' corresponded to Walker's desolate existence and reflected the dehumanisation of modern urban life.[47]

Boorman didn't know the city well, and so he couldn't determine the best locations for his picture. MGM and the union insisted that he rely on the studio's location department. Since Boorman couldn't describe what he wanted without seeing it first, this wouldn't work. The day of the recon, he broke protocol by driving himself, and the location crew followed. After running a few red lights, Boorman shook his handlers, and he explored the interminable labyrinths of concrete alone.[48]

What Boorman found was akin to what Herman Melville discovered in his broodings over whiteness: bright spaces are just as terrifying as dark ones. Contrary to Roman Polanski in his *Chinatown* (1974), Boorman didn't sense in LA the romantic vestiges of 1940s' noir. He apprehended inhuman geometries: car lots lined with glaring metal; propped-up monotonous freeways and their waste spaces underneath; cemeteries where massive machines scoop out identical graves; monolithic skyscrapers blank save uniform rectangular scorings; desert-bleak storm drains; distant viaducts aliens might have erected; wires and more wires gridding sunbaked skies.[49]

5670 Wilshire Blvd

Huntley Hotel

If Boorman's vacant spaces – such as the Huntley Hotel of Second St and California Ave, Santa Monica; the 77-storey office building on 5670 Wilshire Blvd; and the LA River storm drain at Sixth St Bridge – are estranging, they aren't ugly. Following Michelangelo Antonioni in *Il deserto rosso/Red Desert* (1964), where the slow camera elevates Ravenna's wastes to poetry, Boorman liberates sublimity from the concrete. Low-angle shots of blindingly white skyscrapers and wide shots of parched paved distances insinuate infinite yearning. And the blanched rectilinear surfaces recall the surreal multiplications of Escher.

Boorman was the first in a series of post-1950s' European directors to revere Los Angeles in their films. He was followed by Jacques Demy (*Model Shop* [1969]), Antonioni (*Zabriskie Point* [1970]), Jacques Deray (*Un homme est mort/The Outside Man* [1972]) and Roman Polanski (*Chinatown*). Though each director perceives a different Los Angeles, all of them capture an essential dualism that American directors had mostly missed: what makes LA feel so banal, its indifference to tradition, imbues it with exhilarating possibilities. Perhaps it took outsiders from tradition-heavy countries to appreciate the ecstasy of 'anything goes'. Contrast these foreigners' exuberance for the city with Woody Allen's small-minded satire in *Annie Hall* (1977) or Robert Altman's smoggy convolutions in

The Long Goodbye (1973), and laud them for inspiring later filmic odes to LA's lovely vacuities: *The Driver* (1978), *Repo Man* (1984), *Heat* (1995), *Jackie Brown* (1997), *Boogie Nights* (1997), *The Big Lebowski* (1998) and *Drive* (2011).[50]

Point Blank's spatial contrast to Los Angeles is Alcatraz Federal Penitentiary, crepuscular and enclosed where the city is noontime and endless. Filming in LA wrapped in late March of 1967, and the cast and crew moved up the coast to the abandoned prison. It had been shut down since 1963. *Point Blank* would be the first project allowed to film there.

Boorman fixated on the prison's metal. Virtually the first scene in the film shows Walker lying shot in an Alcatraz cell, the shadows of steel bars looming over him. When he finally drags himself out of the cell, networks of cruel metal engulf him – cell bars, railings, catwalks.

Alcatraz

Very soon after, he lies motionless on the rusted iron of the prison's grates or hangs from the barbed wire on the chain-linked fence.

Compared to the rest of the film, the opening in Alcatraz is extremely short, only about 8 per cent of the overall running time. But the prison haunts the movie, its enclosing lines crossing almost every scene. Walker walks out of his dead wife's room and looks through a window screen that resembles a prison fence. He squats in the corner of Lynne's empty apartment, and nearby windowpanes resemble prison bars. The rectangular windows on the Organisation's office building also recall the jail cell, as do the venetian blinds in a mobster's office. But linear imagery isn't the only way Alcatraz pervades the film; the actual prison returns in Walker's many flashbacks. To this traumatised man, almost every event jolts him back to the moment he was gunned down in the empty cell.[51]

Point Blank is an agon between the claustrophobic configurations of Alcatraz and the vacuous surfaces of the city. If the former suggest limbo, the latter intimate vertigo. Is the limbo stasis, or preparation? Is the dizziness disorientation, or liberation? That we must look at shapes to consider these questions implies a moral geometry not unlike the one in Hitchcock's *Psycho* (1960), where modern horizontal designs collide with looming gothic mansards.

* * *

Boorman's interiors also connote through their colours. The director hoped to shoot the movie in black and white, but MGM wanted colour. This would be his first time shooting with the full spectrum at his disposal. Boorman decided to do something quite radical: he would design each scene around one hue. He would begin the film with 'cold colours, greys and blues, then move through the spectrum as the character warmed up, ending in sombre red'.[52] This technique allowed Boorman to film in a colour register with which he was, as a seasoned director of black-and-white, familiar: monochrome. Shooting scenes all in one colour also permitted him to organise and intensify the moods of the film.

The green spectrum

The head of MGM's art department denounced this scheme as
lunacy. He feared that a scene in a green office with green furniture
and seven men in green suits would be laughable at best, unusable at
worst. Boorman defended his plan by reminding the studio that the
greens would not appear as uniform when filmed.[53] Based on their
response to film emulsion, some greens would appear as yellowish,
others close to brown. He was right. In the scene in question you
would never know that everything is green unless someone told you.
You see, in addition to various shades of green, blacks, greys, browns,
yellows, even hints of purple.

The green dictates the mood. In this office of one of the
Organisation's top executives, the negative qualities associated with
green pervade: sickliness, jealousy, envy. Money is also suggested.
That green is most often associated with fertility, health and
creativity proves ironic in this space, where men reduce life to
price tags.

Unlike the unhealthy mobster, Walker changes his colour. He
warms up. The ghostly greys of his meeting with Lynne turn into
sunny yellow once he encounters Chris, and this yellow next blazes
into fierce orange.

Boorman's visual ambitions were high, and he was lucky to
have Philip Lathrop as his cinematographer. Like many on the crew

of *Point Blank*, Lathrop had long been working in the studio system. He had already been nominated for an Academy Award, for *The Americanization of Emily* (1964), and he had shot *Breakfast at Tiffany's* (1961). He was especially adept with the Panavision camera, as he demonstrated to good effect in the wide shots in the Western *Lonely Are the Brave* (1962).

Luckily, Lathrop shared Boorman's taste for innovation. He had in fact operated the camera for one of the most original shots in film history, the twelve-minute take that opens Orson Welles's *Touch of Evil* (1958). Integral to this last great black-and-white noir, Lathrop was perfectly suited to film Boorman's noir in colour. The low light Lathrop shed on Boorman's scenes saturated the already similar shades, creating an eerie semi-uniformity. The opposite of black-and-white's chiaroscuro, which can overwhelm viewers with visual information, Lathrop's dreamily gradated hazes blank the spirit.

The cinematographer's skilful use of the 40mm Panavision created disconcerting wide shots of Walker against the expansive vacancies of Los Angeles. Allowing for excellent depth-of-field, this lens revealed both foreground and background with almost equal clarity. The effect is contradictory. The paved expanses behind Walker press forward, hungry to engulf him, but Walker's lucidity seems a match for the sinister horizon.

The storm drain

Boorman was also fortunate in his editor. Henry Berman was fresh from winning an Academy Award for his work on the 1966 *Grand Prix*, John Frankenheimer's giddy attempt to capture high-speed auto racing on celluloid. The cuts are as quick and bewildering as headlong cubism: a wrench tightens a nut, an exhaust spews smoke, tires burn their rubber, a driver's hands on the wheel, feet on the clutch and gas, hand on the gear shift, medium shot of the Formula One racer skidding into a turn, aerial shot of the whole race, back to the clutch, and so on. All within seconds.

Berman's skill for exhilarating fragmentation served Boorman well, especially in *Point Blank*'s opening sequence, an addled kaleidoscope of flashbacks, jump cuts, cross-cuts, fade-ins. If Berman isn't struggling to capture the outrageous speeds of Formula One, he is out for something a hundred-fold more difficult: tracking the vertiginous movements of a traumatised mind, where time's comforting 'if-then' shatters into the unpredictable 'and … and … and'.

Boorman was also lucky in his composer, Johnny Mandel. Mandel had already won a Grammy for *The Sandpiper* (1965), and he had been nominated for the same award for *I Want to Live!* (1958). He would go on to compose the famous opening score for the television show *M*A*S*H* (CBS, 1972–83), based on his composition for Altman's 1970 film. Like Berman and Lathrop, he embraced Boorman's experimental vibe. To get a feel for the Alcatraz scenes, he wandered through the empty cell blocks. There he came upon an old piano, and he played it. It was out of tune. The discord suited the environment, and it inspired Mandel to compose the score in twelve-tone, Arnold Schoenberg's 'angular and jolting' rebellion against traditional classical music.[54] Through woodwinds, especially flutes, Mandel transformed the disharmonies into eerie whispers, portentous and mournful.

5 What It Is, Is What You See

Point Blank opens with a bright red screen and Mandel's foreboding dissonance. The titles appear – studio, producers – before the red fades into Marvin's face in close-up, flooded in red light. He is bewildered. The camera pulls back before a fade to black. A blast. Another. Gunshots. A man stumbles. Simultaneously, Marvin's name appears, and then the film title, in large white lettering. Now a high-angle medium shot of a man lying on his back in a small dark cement room. Shadows of bars rise up the wall to his right. He wears black. A high-angle close-up follows. Dim light on the man's face. His hands convulse. Then a voiceover – Marvin's voice – hesitant, as if he is first learning to talk. 'Cell … prison cell.' As the voice sounds, a cut to a low-angle shot of the wall to his right – once more the shadows of prison bars. Cut back to Marvin lying wounded, high-angle close-up, another voiceover: 'How did I get here?'

All of this takes place in thirty-five seconds. It's the chaos of birth: into self-awareness. We the audience are thrown into similar turbulence. Why does the film open in harsh red, followed by an unknown man (yes, it's Lee Marvin, but who is he here?) caught baffled in a spooky red light? Who fires the shots, and why? Is the wounded man serving a prison sentence? Which prison is this? Will he die?

After this opening cacophony, the film barely slows, as we watch this wounded man's mind frantically try to piece together a story that is pure Poe: a nameless man lying imprisoned and wounded and alone, not sure how he got there or what's going to happen next.

The film cuts to a crowded party, sweaty middle-aged men in black suits. A harmonica plays mournfully, and a man grabs the man in the prison from behind, calls him 'Walker', punches him and tackles him to the floor. The man is screaming. He needs Walker's help. Walker appears to be drunk.

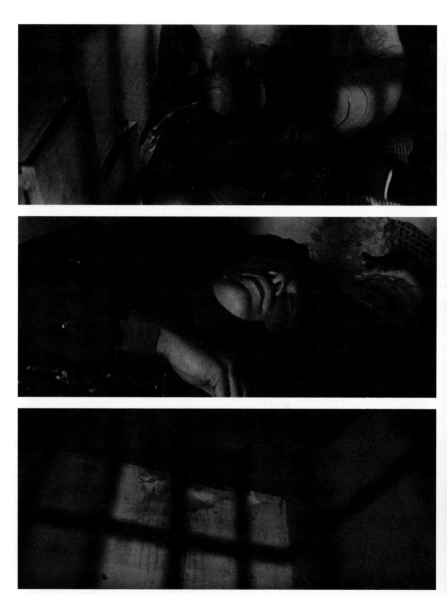

Walker shot; a dying man's face; prison shadows

Cut to a prison. Walker and the man – we soon discover he is Mal – stand on a metal catwalk between two buildings. They are behind a chain-linked fence, and they are dressed in black. A woman stands on the ground below, wearing a grey jacket and scarf. She looks up at the men. A voiceover plays; it is the man who tackled Walker. 'They use the prison,' he says. 'It's closed, we just wait.'

Fade-in to night, the same scene minus the woman, and the voiceover continues, 'We'll just take it from them.' Two men carrying a large steel box appear under the catwalk.

The voiceover: 'You're my friend, Walker.'

Then Walker, also in voiceover, repeats, hesitantly, as if trying to understand, 'My friend.'

Then Mal's voiceover: 'I can't make it on my own.'

And Walker's: 'Help … my friend.'

Cut back to the party, and again Mal and Walker are on the floor, and Mal screams at Walker, 'Trust me!'

The shots again are jarringly quick, taking place within a minute, and again, if this is our first time seeing the film, we can't tell what's going on. Who is who? Where is the prison? Why is the aggressive man in trouble? Are these men professional crooks? What are the men going to take?

But the scenes in this sequence run a bit slower than those in the film's first seconds. The next progression is slower still, and though voiceovers and quick cuts to different locales disorient, a more linear plot grounds us.

Walker, shot on the prison cot, is beginning to make sense of the fragments.

We learn that Mal owes someone a lot of money, and he'll be killed if he doesn't pay. He's set up a job to rob the couriers in a drug drop. The drop takes place at the prison. All he and Walker need to do is knock out the couriers and the money is theirs. But when the action unfolds, Mal shoots the men, after which he hugs Walker and yells, 'We made it!'

Walker pushes him off, replies, 'We blew it!'

The next sequence is the most continuous and slowly paced yet, and it features the first significant appearance of the woman we saw earlier. She is Lynne, Walker's wife. She is tallying the score inside the warden's office – we now know the prison is Alcatraz – while Mal records her figures. Walker paces, says they should get out of here, and Mal commands him to 'shut up!' He's clearly in charge. Walker sulks away, asks Lynne if she's coming, and disappears into the interiors of the prison.

Now we witness the first events that Walker himself is absent from. How can he know what transpires between Mal and Lynne if he isn't near them? Either we must picture a perspective other than Walker's, the cinematic equivalent of the 'third-person omniscient narrator', or we must assume that this scene unfolds as Walker imagines it. Given the acutely subjective nature of the events so far – they are slivers of the traumatised Walker's memory – it is reasonable to choose the latter option. But this means that we can't trust the 'objectivity' of the events. How can Walker be reliable if he's not present?

We learn from the conversation between Mal and Lynne that the money isn't enough to cover Mal's debt. We also see that the two have developed a romantic relationship, and they have concocted a plot against Walker.

Next is the first scene of Walker and Lynne together. In a close-up, Walker lies on his back on a prison cot, and Lynne lies on top, her head resting on his stomach. 'How did we get in this mess?,' she asks. Walker, hesitantly, 'I don't know ... I'. Lynne hums a spooky tune. It echoes through the prison. Is it a signal to Mal?

Mal walks towards the cell. He appears in the door, commands Lynne to come to him. She stands up; Walker does, too. Just as she reaches Mal, he throws her aside and fires twice into Walker's gut. Walker falls back onto the cot. Mal looks ecstatic, orgasmic even. He and Lynne leave. Walker's fingers twitch. The shadows of prison bars appear high on the wall to his right. Back to Walker on the cot, wounded, and his voiceover: 'Did it happen? A dream. A dream.'

Not ten minutes have passed, and we've come full circle, progressing from a man ignorant as a vexed infant to someone who has pieced together a jagged narrative of origin. But already this notion of linear progress is troubled. If we take the chronology of the opening ten minutes seriously, the film begins only seconds after Walker is shot. In that flash, would he have forgotten the events that led to his lying wounded in a cell? And then would he have replayed these events in his mind in only another few seconds?

Since everything in the film seems to have taken place in Walker's mind, how can we know if ensuing events are not also imagined? We can see why some viewers believe that the movie is Walker's dream of revenge as he lay dying in prison – a version of Ambrose Bierce's 'An Occurrence at Owl Creek Bridge'.[55] Boorman himself doesn't endorse this theory. For him, it doesn't matter if Walker's story is real or illusory. 'What [the story] is, is what you see.'[56]

What we see is a narrative far from wish fulfilment. It is fraught with painful flashbacks and concludes with Walker once more playing the dupe. Whatever its status – fact or fantasy – the story that follows is a trauma narrative, a representation of torment and of the effort to work through it.

6 Space and Time

As the credit sequence rolls, Mandel's hypnotic score still sounding, Boorman depicts Walker in a series of ominous tableaux vivants. He is a man in limbo.

Walker struggles to stand just outside the cell where he was shot. Once he is upright, he hunches, holds his gut, freezes.

Staggering over a catwalk of metal grating, Walker stops, lies on his stomach. He holds still.

Walker stands on a metallic jetty. Mangled barbed wire surrounds him. He stares out into San Francisco Bay. It is dawn.

Walker hangs one leg over the top of a chain-linked fence, and one arm over the barbed wire running above. A guard tower looms behind.

When Walker finally gets moving, he stumbles into the frigid bay. This is re-birth, a descent from limbo into the liquid womb. If his survival of the cold water, not to mention his gunshots, seems physically impossible, it is psychologically realistic, a moribund man desperate for animation.

Just as Walker slides into the water, San Francisco within his sights, we hear a woman's voice talking about how the bay has made Alcatraz virtually escape-free. She sounds like a tour guide.

Then, in one of the film's most breathtaking edits, Walker appears on a boat. He looks older (his brown hair is now white) and determined (his gaze is more focused) and sharp (he has traded his robber's duds for a crisp grey suit). He is a new man.

But not really. The boat is touring Alcatraz – the same woman's voice continues to emphasise the impossibility of escape – and the prison appears behind him.

The temporal leap forward from wounded Walker entering deadly waters to a healthy, older Walker floating on them reflects the

Walker rising; the catwalk; chain-linked limbo

character's psyche: since all that matters to him is recovering what Mal took from him, any time period that doesn't pertain to the quest essentially doesn't exist.

The leap in time is matched by the one in space. The tour guide voices over Walker on the shore of Alcatraz and Walker sailing by Alcatraz. He is two places at once, at the site of the trauma and where he tries to heal it.

The remainder of the film is a mash-up of neo-noir thriller and trauma narrative. Like significant neo-noirs of its period – *Chinatown*, *The Long Goodbye*, *Night Moves* (1975) – *Point Blank* expresses classical noir conventions (flawed hero, femme fatale, moral ambiguity) through a post-Hays Code sensibility: lawlessness can go unpunished, sexuality can be raw and violence can be graphic. But if *Point Blank* deals in enigmas, it nonetheless remains true to the basic linear structure of crime thrillers: step-by-step, the protagonist pursues his justice, revenge or money. The instant Walker appears on the tour boat, he pushes relentlessly towards the dough he believes Mal owes him, his $93,000 share of the score. His hard-eyed purposefulness, however, is thwarted by flashbacks to his betrayal, repetitions of its wounds, fears of it happening again. His feet pound forward; his psyche jerks him back.[57]

If Walker's trauma hinders his quest for what's his (though not really; the money is stolen), his drive for the cash exacerbates

The new Walker

his torment. He seems to believe that if he can get his hands on the money, he will be made whole. Boorman himself has said as much: the money is a symbol for the humanity Walker has lost.[58] But Walker's obsession with his money is a diversion from what would make him feel alive again: the ability to transfer his affections for Lynne and Mal to other people. The distraction is understandable: a quest for money that would validate him as a successful man is much easier, even if more physically dangerous, than working through trauma.

*　*　*

The period from Walker's appearance on the boat to his encounters with his wife demonstrates this conflict between violence and recovery. The instant after we see the new Walker, a man appears near him. He is a little older than Walker, probably in his fifties. Like Walker, he wears a suit. While the tour guide describes failed escapes, the man asks, 'How did you make it, Walker?' He is not looking at Walker, nor Walker at him.

The two men stand in another part of the boat, still not facing each other. The man says, 'Using the rock, for a drop.' Walker thinks the man is the police. No, the man is Yost (Keenan Wynn), and he wants to bring the Organisation down. He'll help Walker find his money if Walker will help him undermine the syndicate. Yost knows where Lynne is now living and believes that Mal is there.

We later find out who Yost is, but at this point, we have no idea. And we wonder, how does he know so much about the Alcatraz heist, Walker's wife and friend, and organised crime?

Yost's showing Walker Lynne's address in LA is like a starting gun. Walker stares at it, commits it to memory, turns away and … cut to a stark LAX corridor, and Walker clomping towards a low-angle camera.

There is no more potent rendering of trauma's compressions than this. The boat sailing back to shore, Walker booking a flight to LA, travelling to the airport, flying, landing: all of this is nothing. Only the next decisive step towards the $93,000 is. Walker *walking*

Walker *walking*

so vehemently is Marvin at his most Marvin: his face is etched ferociousness, his body gracefully explosive. He is terrifying.

So indelible was this scene, that when Marvin died and his widow asked Boorman if he would like something of Lee's, he requested the shoes the actor wears here.[59] They are now stored in the Boorman archive at the University of Indiana. They are size thirteen, heavy, well made, impeccably polished.

Boorman intercuts between Marvin striding down the corridor and Lynne waking up in her bed. It's as if the clomps have opened her eyes. The clomps continue as Lynne chooses a dress from her wardrobe, like she's preparing for her husband's arrival. The wardrobe door, like the walls in Lynne's bedroom, is mirrored. Next Lynne applies eye make-up at a mirror in her bathroom. Walker's soles smack.

When Boorman cuts to Walker, now driving to Lynne's apartment, the clomping continues on the soundtrack. Even if Walker is physically no longer in the airport, the fierceness of his pursuit persists. Even after the striding ceases – as it will soon – it echoes in the mind, an elemental reminder of Walker's urgency.

Walker drives a black station wagon with red leather interior. This is a hearse, for Lynne. As Boorman has noted, her dressing and applying make-up are the rituals of a person preparing for death.[60]

Mirrors

After putting on her eye make-up in her apartment, Lynne sits under a hooded hairdryer in a salon. A beautician helps her remove face cream. Facing mirrors create an infinity effect.

Lynne is obsessed with mirrors. The glass emphasises her duplicity and shallowness, tragically on display when she betrayed Walker.

The intercutting between Walker and Lynne and the sound of clomping feet ends when Walker, watching from his car, sees Lynne somnambulistically climb the stairs to her apartment, apparently fresh from the beauty parlour. She moves with uncanny deliberation, reminding the viewer of Maya Deren's day-mare in *Meshes of the Afternoon* (1943). She enters her home.

Walker explodes through her door, gun drawn. He grabs Lynne by the chin, spins her around, pulls her to the floor, rushes into her bedroom, fires six shots into her unmade bed. Impossibly, scorch

Post-coital lassitude

marks surround the bullet holes – symbols of the futility of Walker's violence. He rushes into the bathroom, rifles through the cosmetics. No proof of a man living here.

He returns to the living room, sits on the couch, empties his shells on the coffee table, leans back. He is silent, exhausted. He stares indifferently ahead. (Boorman, remember, said this lassitude was post-coital.) Then, as if in a trance, Lynne answers the questions Walker doesn't articulate. Mal has been gone for three months. She's glad Walker's alive. She can't sleep, takes pills, dreams about Walker being dead, wishes she were dead. She survives on the $1,000 a month Mal sends. He pays for the apartment.

The apartment, its décor, the clothing of Walker and Lynne: all are a shade of grey. Both characters are ghostly, drained of emotion. But the grey is also the fog from which anything might emerge. Walker will arise from the mist more animated. Lynne dissolves.

The lifelessness of the scene feels more devastating when Lynne recounts the day she and Walker first met. As she speaks, we witness the event in a flashback. Walker is younger, with brown hair, and he wears a dark green jacket. He strolls along a harbour. Is he a longshoreman? He is smiling, relaxed, playful, hands in his back pockets, like a little boy.[61] Other men surround him, also jovial, perhaps fellow workers. It is raining. Lynne walks the harbour just in front of Walker. They're both a little drunk.

A delightful flirtation ensues. Walker nears Lynne; he is shy, vulnerable, but also goofily charming. Wearing a sky-blue outfit, she glances at him out of the corner of her eye, hints interest, turns from him. Then she lets down her hair. She faces him and stares, surprised at her boldness. As the characters tentatively circle each other, grinning, Walker gives the smallest, gentlest bow, an act so humble and hammy and cocky, it wins Lynne that instant. The two continue to circle, awkwardly preening. The other men stand by and laugh. Everyone is having a fantastic time, and Walker, of all people, is the master of this little outbreak of revels. As Lynne herself says, he was funny when he was drunk. She doesn't remember his

The rondure of courting

quips from that day, but suddenly they were together, and we watch the two of them some time later walking into the ocean, Lynne in a one-piece the same light blue as her outfit, Walker in a bathing-suit loudly patterned in orange, yellow and red flowers. They dive into a wave.

We've not seen this Walker before, and we aren't likely to again. How could such a lumbering sweetheart freeze into this icy stalker? Will we ever catch a flash of humour again, or a gesture of alluring vulnerability?[62]

The potential exists, and it suggests a third Walker persona. The first lies wounded in the Alcatraz cell. The second stomps forward in LAX. And now we have the loopy lover, whose re-emergence would mock the tough guy and minister to the wounded. This third identity hovers as an agonising 'what-if' (what if Mal had never come along?) and the smallest of hopes (for a return of the harbour clown).

Into Lynne's narrative, Mal thrusts. Still in the flashback, Walker and Mal, old friends long absent from each other, reunite. Lynne, Walker and Mal become inseparable. Lynne hovers happily between the two men, until she floats towards Mal.

Lynne's story stops. Walker sits alone on her couch. Night has fallen, and his face is no longer rigid. It is pliable, pained. Lynne retires to her bedroom. Walker sleeps on the couch.

In what appears to be a dream, he relives his explosion into Lynne's bedroom. This time, he shoots the bed in slow motion. An exaggerated recoil reveals the futility of his revenge. He is impotent, and examples of his weakness relentlessly repeat.

Awakened by the dream, Walker enters Lynne's bedroom. She is dead. An empty pill bottle on her bedstand explains it all. Walker leans towards her as though – so the script indicates[63] – he is going to kiss her. Instead, he ruefully places his wedding ring on her finger, the golden circle now a cruel parody of the couple's joyous courting rondure.

The following scenes confirm the film as a manifestation of Walker's damaged psyche. He rushes out of the bedroom, stands bewildered in the middle of the living room, moves to a window and jerks the curtain aside.

Cut to Walker's point of view, and the window screen looks like prison bars, and there is Yost not thirty feet from the window, leaning against a black car. He waves. The screen bars fade away before a close-up on Walker's troubled face. He hears the eerie tune Lynne hummed in the prison, just before Mal shot him.

Walker returns to the bedroom. It is empty, save a bed with a bare mattress and a bedstand with nothing on it. The humming stops. A white cat sits on the mattress, over which bar-like shadows fall. The creature runs away. Walker enters the bathroom; Lynne's things remain. He picks up a large bottle of green liquid, drops it into the bathtub. It shatters, and the green flows among the colours of other spilled soaps, perfumes, unguents. According to Boorman, these slowly mixing liquids are Lynne's life ebbing away. The humming begins again.

This remarkable sequence shows that though Walker is no longer physically in Alcatraz, he remains in the prison of his trauma. Also, we realise that Yost possesses a preternatural knowledge of Walker's goings-on. (Boorman likened him to Merlin the Magician.[64]) Moreover, we understand, once again, that linear time and continuous space are meaningless to the victim of trauma. The time between Lynne's death and the removal of her body has vanished,

Another prison; a jump in time; life ebbs away

More incarceration

just as the gradual transformation of the space has been chopped into discontinuous chunks. Only the events connected to Walker's angst – his discovery of her body, the grim realisation that the world is empty of her, her spooky humming – matter.

A similar compression occurs when Walker exits the bathroom. The living room, furnished and decorated when Walker entered Lynne's room, is bare. Lynne's humming continues. Walker moves to a corner and squats. Shutters on either wall resemble prison bars. The humming morphs into Mal's voice commanding Lynne to come to him, and a gun blasts. The sound of Walker falling in the prison cell blurs into a rapping at the door, and Walker stands. He has traded his grey suit for a blue one. The living room is furnished once more. The world no longer feels as empty to Walker as it did, so objects have returned. He has a plan for finding Mal. He will interrogate the man who delivers the monthly cheque to Lynne. It is he who knocks.

Walker again explodes at the door. He roughs up the delivery guy, gets the information he wants: a John Stegman (Michael Strong) arranges the money drops. He might lead to Mal.

7 The Movie House

From his interrogation of Stegman onward, we see Walker's comic persona gain force. The comedy satirises traditional masculinity by fomenting violence so extreme it looks ridiculous. That Walker's hyperbolic violence never actually kills anyone, that it is often directed towards machines immune to suffering: both suggest that the violence is moreover impotent. Walker would know: his own efforts to bring about healing through violence are futile.

As is his quest to become whole through gaining his $93,000. The equation of this monetary amount and his recovery of his masculinity is another satirical strain in the film. The Organisation is criminalised capitalism. The bad guys are men in expensive suits and sleek offices, and their profits take the forms of credit cards and stock portfolios. A man's worth in this outfit is measured by his wealth and ability to manage wealth. Mal stole Walker's share of the heist to buy his way back into the group (he had earlier botched a transaction) and now he is trying to demonstrate his corporate viability. For Walker to attach his own worth to $93,000 is absurdly ironic: he reinforces the syndicate he's bent on bringing down.

Big John Stegman's car lot – located at 8855 West Washington Blvd in Culver City – is all scorched metal, sleazy salesmen, creepy womanising. Stegman struts across his lot, self-satisfied and in charge, leering at an attractive blonde in a tight minidress. Walker appears out of nowhere. He wants to buy the Chrysler Imperial Crown Convertible, a luxury car. The men head out for a test drive.

Walker pretends interest in the car. 'Pretty nice rig,' he announces, playing the role, a little over-the-top, of the car dealer's mark. Walker fastens his seat belt. When the don't-play-by-the-rules Stegman says Walker doesn't have to do this, Walker, again perfectly

The test drive

performing the chump, announces that 'Most accidents take place within three miles of home.'

On the road, Stegman turns on the radio to hear the ad for his business. Without warning Walker veers into the other lane and off the road, and he's no longer playing the dupe. He guns the car, slams the brakes, whiplashes the unbelted Stegman. Does it again. Walker demands to know where Mal is. Stegman won't squawk. Walker speeds into a littered wasteland beneath a highway underpass. He bashes head-on into a pile, puts the car in reverse, crashes back into another pile, repeats. Stegman bangs the dash, the windscreen. Walker presses Stegman on Mal, and Stegman mocks Walker about Mal taking his wife, and he blusters about Mal 'nailing' Lynne's sister Chris, too. Walker keeps up the vicious driving. He caves in the front and back of the car and shreds the top. The passenger's door pops open, out tumbles the battered Stegman. Walker is on him, shaking him by his lapels. Stegman won't give up Mal, but he tells Walker where Chris works, a jazz club called The Movie House. Walker strides away. Stegman tries to close the ruined door. A bum living under the overpass approaches.

Take away the dialogue and turn it black and white, this scene could appear in a Keystone slapstick. The slick dealer gets his comeuppance from the potential victim, who, instead of beating up the confidence man, roughs up his most valuable product. Comedy aside, Walker's attack on the Chrysler implies an equation between Stegman and machine: knocking one around is the same as knocking the other around. What makes Stegman mechanistic is what makes all Organisation men mechanistic: they are parts in a vast money-making system, useful only so long as they contribute, disposable when they don't.[65]

* * *

Boorman cuts from the bewildered Stegman to another scene highlighting the mechanistic dangers of American capitalism. Walker stands in close-up on a green sward, the LA freeways swarming in the distance. He looks down. His wife's gravestone. He's in a cemetery, Forest Lawn Memorial Park. Nearby, a huge excavator digs a grave, just as it scooped out Lynne's. For Boorman, this machine sums up American life – its dehumanising corporatisation. 'It used to be that, no matter how useless your life had been, it would at least give a gravedigger a day's work to dig your grave.' Now, to have your plot excavated in ten minutes with a 'mechanical spade': this is the 'greatest of all betrayals'.[66]

Boorman's America also flattens men into images, simulations. After a scene (imagined by Walker?) in which Stegman tells Mal that Walker is after him, and Mal orders Stegman to kill Walker, we find Walker in Chris's club. The place is pell-mell: R&B venue, psychedelia, strip joint, mob hangout. On the stage, dimly lighted like the whole place, a Black man wearing all black, including black shades, stands in the middle of a movie screen.[67] He screams. 'Yeah! Yeah!' A projected

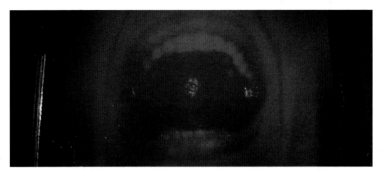

Collapse of dimensions

image of a huge mouth surrounds him. It's as if the singer has backed into the illusion, and the image has thrust forwards into reality. With background and foreground collapsed, it's hard to tell what's fact and what's fantasy. The man continues to scream. The image changes to a Renaissance painting. The singer (he's Stu Gardner and the song is 'Mighty Good Times') moves onto the middle of the stage, in front of his backing band. Images continue to flash on the screen to his left, alternating between blonde-haired women and classical paintings. Green light saturates the pictures, and then red, and green again, and so on. A go-go dancer in bra and panties jiggles to Gardner's right. He jumps off the stage. Plump white men in black suits crowd the front row. They probably work for the Organisation. The singer invites two of them to mimic his screaming. They sheepishly squawk. The epitome of square, they can only let loose if scripted.

Meanwhile, Walker gets Chris's address from a waitress, from whom he learns that there are men in the club looking for him. He leaves through the back way. Just before he exits, he grabs a beer bottle for a weapon. One of Stegman's goons follows him, and another is posted backstage. They attack, and the fight that goes down is brutal, desperate, awkward. The winner will not be the best fighter but the most ruthless, and that's Walker, who takes one man out by punching him viciously in the groin. When the go-go dancer

Part of the show

realises a fight is going on behind her, she screams. But since the
singer and the audience are screaming, no one can tell that anything's
wrong. Walker wanders from backstage into the red light. This is the
first scene of the film, just before Walker is shot by Mal. He squints,
pained and confused. To the audience, he's only another performer,
perhaps experiencing stage fright.

In The Movie House, the distinction between substance and
semblance is lost. This is why Walker looks so distraught: a major
moment in his quest to recover his vitality is not even viewed as
real. That Boorman begins *Point Blank* with this scene suggests that
Walker's true quest is not the $93,000 but a life beyond simulation.

8 Golden Androgyny

If there is in *Point Blank* an episode showing Walker breaking out of type, it occurs right after his scuffle at the jazz club. Bruised and battered, he arrives at Chris's apartment. Unlike the other buildings in Boorman's LA, its exterior is made of wood, and it's surrounded by trees. An experienced thief, Walker breaks in easily, takes out his gun. We are on the verge, it appears, of a repeat of the break-in at Lynne's apartment. Maybe Mal is here. Will Walker rush to the bedroom and open fire?

He does enter the bedroom, and he finds a woman sleeping there. He tries to wake her, but she's out. Dead like Lynne? He turns on the bedstand light. Flowers decorate the shade, and above the bed hangs a piece of modern art, rich in yellows, golds, creams and browns. The wall itself is honey yellow. This is not the ghostly dwelling of Walker's dead wife. But is it just as tragic? Walker finds a pill bottle beside the bed. He sits on the edge of the mattress and tries to rouse the woman again. She wakes up, groggy. 'Walker,' she says, gently. It's Chris, and she is not afraid.

Walker gets to the point. 'Where's Mal?' His voice is hard. Not quite cognisant, Chris ignores the question. Drowsily, she tells Walker he's 'supposed to be dead'. No, he says, Lynne is dead. Pills. He slaps the bottle off the bedstand with the barrel of his .44. Chris says she's not been sleeping.

If you care about Walker's character by this point in the film, the next lines are heartbreaking. Walker says he's heard that Chris is with Mal. 'No,' she replies. 'Why don't you want him?' he asks. She answers: 'Because he makes my flesh crawl.' 'I want him,' Walker says. Then, in a film of brutally efficient dialogue and dead-eyed stares, an exquisitely delicate line rises, uncalled for, tangential, uttered by a woman vulnerable in her sleepiness, wearing a soft white T-shirt,

Another perspective

but also sexy, relaxed and welcoming in her bed. Chris says, 'You
were always the best thing about Lynne.'

In that sentence exists an alternative universe, as far from
criminal LA as Lynne's sterile little palace is from Chris's pastoral
interiors. The sentence implies that Walker had affectionate relations
beyond his treacherous wife and friend. His sister-in-law liked him.
And why not? From what we saw in Walker's first encounter with
Lynne, he was loose, gallant, tender, handsome.

It's not only what Dickinson's Chris says to Walker. It's how she
says it. So spontaneously, casually, with no ulterior motive, nothing
to gain. This in a world where everyone's out for something, trying to
reduce you to a means for their furtherance.

In confessing to Walker that he was the best thing about Lynne,
Chris offers him succour that he has not experienced, at least since
he was shot. And how does Walker respond? He doesn't. As if Chris
said nothing, he asks *why* she doesn't want Mal. He is paranoid. All
women, especially the sister of his unfaithful wife, are surely bent
on betraying him with Mal. Mercifully, Chris doesn't show any
disappointment over this implied accusation. She tells Walker that she
doesn't want *any* member of the Organisation. This outfit killed her
boyfriend, took over his club and forces her to run it. She says that
she loved her boyfriend. To which Walker, like an automaton unable

to understand basic human feelings, replies, 'Why?' Alert to his emotional stupidity, Chris answers in kind: 'Hey, gotta make a living.'

During this conversation, Walker has sat on the edge of Chris's bed. The camera has hovered just over his shoulder, looking down at her. The effect falls somewhere between a point-of-view perspective and a more objective one. It is a relief to feel that we aren't limited solely to Walker's angle. There is room for expansion, both for the audience and maybe for Walker himself. If anyone can lift Walker out of his tormented ego to see through someone else's eyes, it is Chris.

* * *

The next cut is harsh: the Organisation's Wilshire Blvd high-rise office building, filmed from a low angle, blinding white, redundant window patterns chopping its concrete into immense prison bars. As the starkness offends the eye, unseen engines (jackhammers?) trouble the ear. In terms of plot, the brief scene that takes place within the building is inconsequential: Stegman reports to a furious Mal that Walker lives. We already know Walker escaped The Movie House, and we would assume that Mal would be incensed. Why did Boorman include the scene? To contrast Chris's organic abode with the Organisation's ominous artifices.

In twenty-three seconds, we are back in Chris's apartment and … what seems a different movie. It is morning, and Walker is lounging in a golden robe, and nothing else. Perhaps it's a robe that belonged to Chris's departed lover, but it could well be hers. Well, why wouldn't it be hers? Walker appears to be going full female. He's putting on make-up. Trying to cover a bruise below his eye. The look on his face is whimsical, and he is 'toying', the script says, with the compact case.[68] Any minute he might become Cary Grant in *Bringing Up Baby* (1939), who, while donning a flouncy robe when his clothes are being cleaned, whoops that he's just not himself today.

How did this happen? Has Chris's house relaxed Walker back into his old playfulness? Has she led him into an alternate world where his trauma never occurred? Has she inspired a new identity?

Toying with the compact case

Up until now, Walker has worn only tight, creaseless suits (Boorman wanted them to resemble body armour), and his face has barely cracked into any expression. Now he's loose. His privates might flop out at any minute. Maybe he's tired of performing traditional manhood, with its violence and greed. He's seen how absurd it is to sacrifice the dishevelled frolic of life to the geometries of power. He's ready to cultivate that part of himself the vicious world of men has left him almost bereft of, that part that Boorman observed in Marvin himself: as 'tender ... as a woman's ... to the wounds of the world'.[69]

But these explanations are so serious. Maybe Walker threw on Chris's robe just for the hell of it, and he likes how it feels on his skin, and that bruise looks pretty nasty, so why not grab that make-up kit and hide it?

Regardless of Walker's reasoning, the scene is amiably domestic. It's as though Walker and Chris are married. In her lush golden dress, Dickinson scurries around the apartment gathering things for work. Art hangs on the warm honey walls and the surfaces of the wooden furniture teem with knick-knacks. A tall shelf filled with books covers one wall. An array of hats decorates the wall at the bottom of the stairs.

The scene could indeed be from a Hawks screwball comedy, or maybe a Hudson/Day romcom, or even one of Nick and Nora's

Thin Man movies (1934–47). After enduring Boorman's cruel wastes, we are glad to lounge in this soft, fertile, inconsequential world.

Then, just like that, Walker locks back into auto-mode: get my money, get my money. To Chris's pleasant reminder that they'll meet at noon – as if they have a romantic lunch planned – Walker, in his calloused baritone, booms, 'Don't get lost' – meaning, don't duck out on me, make sure you help me get Mal. Chris is offended. She sensed a softening in Walker, and she responded in kind, and now he's returned to his egotistical quest, and rejects her affection.

* * *

Boorman cuts again to the Organisation's Wilshire high-rise. This time, he shows the interiors, which might be offices in *Mad Men* (AMC, 2007–15). This is crime as everyday corporate capitalism, which means that the Organisation conceals its nefarious dealings (under the name of Multiplex Products) extremely well, but also implies that all corporate capitalism, in viewing humans solely as units of getting and spending, might be criminal.

Mal waits to see Carter (Lloyd Bochner), his superior. He needs help eliminating Walker. Typewriters, ringing phones, professional murmurs are in the background. A smartly dressed receptionist calls Mal back. On the way to Carter's office, Mal is frisked – just routine. And then into Carter's all green room: walls, carpet, phones,

Cold as death

intercom, desk, suit, briefcase, chair, couch. The colour is both ironic
– this world opposes the organic – and accurate: it is diseased. The
décor, highly artificial and minimalist, is cold as death. Carter is the
blandest crime boss imaginable: an efficient businessman giving a
wayward employee, Mal, a self-satisfied talking-to about his unsound
method and proposing a more efficient one. Let Walker know where
Mal is, and he will come for him, and we will eliminate Walker.

While Mal takes his dressing-down, Walker hovers between
his traumatic repetitions and new possibilities. He sits on a
curb stop in a parking lot. Behind him is Ocean Ave in Santa Monica,
behind which is a bluff lined with pine trees. The ocean is beyond.
Walker wears a golden-rust shirt and a lighter golden tie, with a
brown houndstooth coat. These colours suggest vitality, as does
the ocean.

Chris in her lovely honey-yellow dress sits down beside him,
and we recall her exuberantly golden world, and realise: Walker is
dressing like she does. He wants to be a part of her world. (That
Walker never carries a suitcase but wears a variety of elegant
well-tailored suits is part of the film's dreaminess.) She's been out
gathering information, and she tells him of the Organisation's plan,
the setup.

Chris and Walker spend the afternoon figuring out how to
sneak Walker into Mal's penthouse in the Huntley Hotel. Walker
once more plays a more traditionally feminine role. Chris drives his
black station wagon – now more suggestive of a family car than a
hearse – while Walker is the passenger. They gaze up at the Huntley,
its glaring white concrete the same as that of the Wilshire building:
pitiless, impenetrable. Organisation men are everywhere.

Their recon over, Walker and Chris once more position
themselves near the shore of the Pacific. Walker stands beside a bright
yellow coin telescope pointed towards the sea. Put in your dime, gaze
at the waves. Walker wrenches the lens towards the Huntley. The
lock pops with a satisfying 'ping'.[70] He bends down to the level of the
eyepiece and studies Mal's lair.

Lost possibilities

Boorman intercuts between Walker seeing and what Walker sees. One shot is the most compelling of the film: a medium shot of Walker from head-on, the yellow viewfinder covering his face, his body leaned casually back against a waist-high chain-linked fence, the Pacific coruscating in the distance. As with the scene when Walker applies make-up while wearing Chris's robe, this intimates another life. The yellow of the telescope is daffodil, a perfect complement to Walker's golden-rod garb, and the ocean is blue plenitude. All Walker need do is turn around and contemplate the expanding azure. Then what? Through the festive yellow, he might perceive as Chris does, become attuned to play and spontaneity (she is a jazz fan), and he might realise that there are no perfectly straight lines in nature but eddies and waves. He might celebrate his own lively mixes of flux and form.

But Walker keeps his eye on the building, and on his quest, and, worse, uses Chris as a tool to get his money. He asks her how bad Mal wants her. Pretty bad, she admits. Bad enough, he wonders, to let her into the Huntley?

'Why should I?' Chris, angry, asks.

'Well, that's up to you.'

Chris hesitates. But she agrees. She will convince Mal to let her into his penthouse by giving him the impression that she will have sex with him. Once inside, she will unlock the balcony door for Walker. To make the plan believable, she must be willing to go through with the sex, even though Mal makes her flesh crawl. What if Walker doesn't get into the room soon enough? She will have whored herself out for a man she barely knows so he can (possibly) get money that he stole in the first place.

Alexander Jacobs was concerned that audiences wouldn't find Chris's decision convincing. He said a strong intimacy between her and Walker must be established for her choice to make sense.[71] To Jacobs's chagrin, this did not happen, at least not overtly. But the affection is implied in Chris's delicate welcome of Walker into her life, a welcome that awakens desirable traits long latent in the man – offbeat charisma, alluring vulnerability.

But Chris probably has other reasons for going along with Walker's scheme. Maybe she feels guilt for what her sister did to him. Maybe she herself wants Mal to go down.

Perhaps Chris teams with Walker, though, for no clear rationale. She agrees to the plan simply because *she agrees to the plan*. As we know, Boorman's minimalist, fragmented film often leaves out explanations for why things happen. Why does Walker wear a different suit in almost every scene? Where does he sleep? How did he survive his wounds? We don't know, can't know. The mystery applies to Chris's choice. We can surmise why she does it, but we can also say, she simply does it.

And isn't this how so much of life is? Things happen because they happen, and after the fact we try to account for why and how, and we might come up with valid explanations, but we can never know if they're valid once and for all. Does this mean we stop trying to explain? No. We need explanations. But do we settle on one interpretation? No. The world's too inscrutable. At so many junctures, *Point Blank* puts us in this troubling yet generative tension between 'that's it' and 'maybe not'.

***

On Walker's behalf, Chris enters Mal's keep. Night has come, and she wears a golden wool trench coat cut just above the knees. In the lobby of the Huntley the men leer at her. She rides the elevator up.

Meanwhile Walker stands in an apartment window across the street from Mal's building. He has coerced the two inhabitants, seemingly a gay couple, into tying each other up. They will call the police and report being attacked. The police will arrive and divert Mal's guards, and Walker will slip through.

Walker's interactions with the couple are funny. He lounges in a chair, and the two men relax on the couch. It's like they've been casually chatting. When Walker impassively asks them to tie each other up, they do so almost willingly, like they are trying to please their captor. The same is true when one of the men calls the police and reports terrible danger. The other man asks, 'Is that alright?' A deadpan Walker says, 'That's fine. Thank you.' He leaves. The men look at each other excitedly. The whole sequence feels more like broad comedy than suspense.

Not so in Mal's penthouse, where Chris finds herself in a dark fairytale, pitting her nature magic against Bluebeard. Mal's world is crimson: carpets, walls, pillow, robe. Unaware how gross and creepy he is, Mal fashions himself a red-hot lover. When Chris arrives, he stands in his bathroom wearing only brown slacks. He is flabby and hirsute. Soft jazz plays on the stereo. 'C'mon on in, honey!' he says,

The crimson lair

trying to sound authoritative and seductive. He emerges from the bathroom in a too-tight mustard-coloured velour shirt, pours Chris a scotch, and demands that she travel with him to New York. Right after the two sit on the couch, he opens her dress (yellow, again, with golden stripes, a honeybee look); but before he can remove her bra, she hugs him, defensively. Sensing Mal's disappointment, she removes the belt around her dress. Mal grins in ogreish lust.

A siren sounds.

If Mal's efforts are stomach-turningly awkward, Walker's are the opposite. As Mal's guards scramble to figure out why all these cops are showing up, Walker strolls into the Huntley with disarming nonchalance – Marvin, once more, at his most Marvin. Chris has stealthily unlocked the sliding-glass door leading onto the balcony. Without us even seeing, as if he did it effortlessly, Walker has tied up the balcony guards. Mal has got Chris into bed, she's wearing nothing but her slip, and he's getting ready to make his final move – when under the curtains covering the balcony door a hand appears, and it silently lifts the fabric, which bunches like an accordion, and then the .44 emerges. Walker. He passes through. Chris sees him and Walker puts his hand gently on Mal's shoulder and puts his gun to his old friend's head and Chris slaps Mal and screams, 'Get off!'

Walker grabs Mal, still wrapped in his sheet, and drags him to the floor. Walker then clutches the sheet right at Mal's chest and pulls him up. While Walker interrogates Mal about the money, Mal continually falls and Walker jerks him up. Mal is sweating, he can't remember anything. He begs to put his clothes on. Nothing doing, Walker says, you're going with me right now, to see Carter and help me get my money. Walker guides the sheeted Mal onto the balcony; they're going to take the service elevator. 'I'll get your money,' Mal says. 'Trust me!'

This moment is sexual – the way Walker leads the naked Mal around by a sheet bunched in front like a phallus. The early shots of their wrestling on the floor of the party, of Mal looking sexually aroused after shooting Walker, of Walker showing more interest

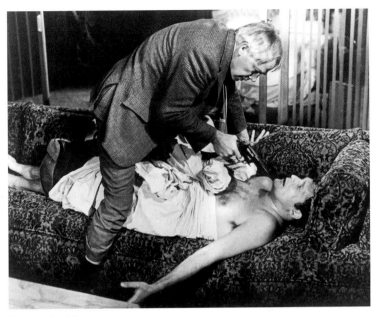

Homoerotic violence

in Mal than the seductive Chris: these all suggest a homoerotic relationship. Not that the two men were lovers. Boorman illuminates the eroticism of violence: in the hypermasculine world of criminalised capitalism, the intimacy of inflicting pain on another man satisfies more than the love embrace.[72]

Walker's (figurative) lovemaking to Mal suffers a coitus interruptus: a flashback. The film cuts to the early moment when Mal tackles Walker to the floor and screams 'Trust me ... you're my friend, Walker, my best friend!'

Back in the present, Walker falters. 'You ... you ...' he stammers. But he recovers fast. He tells Mal that they'll do it together this time, they'll go to Carter, they will get the $93,000.

A light flips on back in the room, and someone calls 'Mal!' It is one of the guards who was standing outside the interior door.

Walker jerks Mal further out onto the balcony. Mal uses the momentum to unravel from the sheet and he falls over the ledge naked and is killed.

With cops now swarming the Huntley – what caused the naked man to fall? – Mal's guards are even more preoccupied, and Walker exits as smoothly as he entered. He finds Chris on the street, tells her Mal fell. Chris is shocked. He fell? 'You should've killed him. You owed it to yourself.'

As if she said nothing, Walker produces the $1,000 that he took from Lynne's delivery boy and says, 'This money belonged to your sister; you'd better take it.'

Offended, Chris replies, 'You died at Alcatraz all right. Goodbye Walker.' Walker barely hears her. He's picking up the payphone to call Carter's office.

Walker is dead to Chris because he didn't want to take revenge on Mal. Even if vengefulness isn't the noblest of human traits, at least it is understandable – if you hurt me, I'll hurt you back – and it is passionate. Some might even believe that revenge is a rough vehicle of justice. But to be indifferent to those who have grossly wronged you – this is inhuman, a psychopathic numbness.

Vengeance would not only have humanised Walker; it would have rendered Chris's sacrifice more meaningful. She risked rape so a man could get $93,000. Now, in offering her Lynne's money, Walker's implied she's a prostitute. This is your fee for seducing Mal.

If Walker showed signs of coming to life earlier in the day, he's now reverted to his hard-as-nails persona, even if he still wears the gold and brown suit that matches him with Chris. The flashback of betrayal that he suffered while he was frisking Mal – this numbed his heart. In once more enduring Mal's villainy, he behaves like Mal. If being a victim is terrible, then being an oppressor might be the opposite, so why not be like the oppressor? Why not treat Chris just as Mal did, as an object?

9 Ironic Genre

Yost appears the instant Chris walks away. He can help Walker find Carter. Cut to some sort of political rally. Everyone is well-dressed, white, middle class, and there is Carter, gladhanding and wearing a badge that reads 'Official'. His wife is with him, young and attractive. Walker appears. Carter struggles to hold his hypocritical blandness together as Walker tells him he'll kill him if he doesn't get his money in twelve hours.

Next we see Carter undone: screaming at his men for letting Walker get to Mal. He is in his green office, and all six men, in the infamous scene, are wearing green of one shade or another. It's funny: the hyper-controlled boss now ranting impotently at his bumbling employees.

Carter plans a setup. He'll send Stegman to give Walker his money near the Sixth St Viaduct in the LA River storm drain (cinematically iconic, featured in *Grease* [1978], *To Live and Die in L.A.* [1985] and *Terminator 2: Judgment Day* [1991]). But unbeknownst to Stegman, it's a setup. A hitman with a rifle will pick him, and Walker, off.

Walker is on to the scheme, however. From a building across the street, he watches Stegman leave the Wilshire high-rise. He crosses a catwalk to the Wilshire offices. White columns spaced every ten feet or so suggest more prison bars. Walker enters and ascends to Carter's office. He is wearing green now himself – behaving as the criminals he is trying to bring down. He leans down to the receptionist, whispers something threatening in her ear, reaches down, unplugs the phone cord, crushes the cord's metal casing with his foot, and orders the receptionist to buzz him in. He rushes through the door, knocks the guard out with his pistol, storms into Carter's office. He wants his money!

Walker forces Carter to drive to the drop-off point. When they arrive, they park in a tunnel leading to the drain. Stegman is below. He holds the package that contains, so he believes, the $93,000. He stands alone in the concrete cavern, a ten-foot wide current of run-off drifting through the drain's bottom. The viaduct hovers above. A train screams on the tracks running parallel to the drain. Walker commands Carter to retrieve the money, pushes him down the incline. 'No, no it's alright!' Carter screams. It's not. The sniper, perched at the top of the opposite incline, a hundred yards off, near the Fourth St Bridge, drops Carter with one shot. Stegman makes a break for it. He goes down, too. Walker watches the carnage from the tunnel.

Cut to the hitman (James Sikking), from whose point of view we've seen Carter and Stegman die. He's dressed like Carter – well-pressed business suit – but not likely to get flustered. With professional detachment, he steps away from his spot, stows his rifle in his trunk and takes out his pipe. He drives away.

This is a world of such loud mechanical noises – trains, cars – that a man can fire a rifle in broad daylight, and no one will notice. It's as if there are no humans around to listen, or to see. Or to feel. Barely a minute after Carter and Stegman are killed, Walker ventures down to the water. He indifferently inspects Carter, finds an address book. Stegman, he ignores. With his gun, he punches the package. No money here, only paper slips. He kicks the package into the water; it floats away. Reversing his camera angle, Boorman reveals Walker in a long shot (see p. 35). The sniper's vantage at Fourth St Bridge looms in the background. In the sweltering distance bland skyscrapers shimmer like ghosts. Radio towers line the gulley sides like monstrous barbed wire. Walker might be the last man on earth.

* * *

One of the pleasures of genre crime fiction is that characters don't learn and change. Marlowe stays Marlowe in Chandler's noirish tales; same with Hammett's Spade. And, of course, Stark's Parker. We enjoy these characters, in book and movie versions, because they are compelling *and* predictable, like a favourite song. Certain movie stars, those who tend to play the same role from picture to picture, embody this pleasing combination. We watch a Bogart film to see Bogart – not an actor (like Daniel Day-Lewis) who disappears into a character. Same goes for other performers who figured out how to be comforting and titillating at once: Cary Grant, say, both Hepburns, George Clooney, Denzel Washington, Julia Roberts.

And Lee Marvin. Aside from his few comic turns (*Paint Your Wagon* [1969], *Cat Ballou*) and his earlier villainy, Marvin plays the same laconic, sardonic hero from film to film, and that through-line is appealing. It's as if he's the main character in the genre called 'Lee Marvin Movie'.

As sangfroid badass, Walker often plays 'Lee Marvin'. But the distressed Walker sometimes misses Marvin's characteristic nonchalance. Not only that: Walker can be outright truculent. And just when we think he might be able to transcend his boorishness – namely in his interactions with Chris – it grips him more tightly.

But if Walker isn't full-on 'Marvin', he's not simply a failed 'Lee'. He hovers between genre virtuosity and something else: an individual, irreducible to type, flawed, yes, but potent, hovering tragically (yet hopefully) between obsession and plasticity, violence and love.

Walker epitomises *Point Blank*'s irony: it is both generic and original. Like Stanley Kubrick's *2001: A Space Odyssey* (1968), Polanski's *Chinatown*, Ridley Scott's *Blade Runner* (1982) and Quentin Tarantino's *Kill Bill* (2003–4), *Point Blank*, through its familiar pop cultural signs, invites viewers into its world. But inside the world, the markers vanish, and we find ourselves in a disturbing space whose rules shift the instant we think we've got them figured. The Russian Formalists call this 'poetic' effect the defamiliarisation of the unfamiliar. We also call it – this abrupt severing of territory and map – enchantment.[73]

Walker's vacillation between familiar and strange might make him more engaging than either extreme alone, but the mixture also turns his character acutely ambiguous. Just when we think he's solidified into *this*, he softens into *that*. And vice versa. We can't predict when he will shift, nor can we explain why. It happens.

All of this is a preamble for the last quarter of *Point Blank*, during which Walker's behaviour, already erratic, becomes bafflingly capricious. Did Boorman not know how to end his film? Or are the last frames rapture?

10 Neurotic Inertia

After the long shot of Walker alone by the gulley's creek, Boorman cuts to Walker and Yost standing beside a swimming pool. Walker wants the next in command, Brewster. Yost tells him that Brewster lives in the large ranch-style house attached to this pool and that the man will be arriving tomorrow morning.

Yost exits, and Walker turns to look out over Hollywood Blvd. The view, from 7655 Curson Terrace, is spectacular. (The Beatles rented the house in August 1966.) But Walker looks troubled, just like he did while staring in the red light at The Movie House. Momentarily drained of his fanatical energy, he faces facts: he is broken and lonely, and even if he gets his money, he will be broken and lonely.

What happens next feels random: Walker drives to Chris's apartment. After their angry and ostensibly final parting after Mal's death, it is odd that Walker would seek her out. And why now? Why didn't he go see her before heading to the viaduct? He had twelve hours. Furthermore, in a film in which Walker simply materialises at his various destinations, as if by magic, why are we now watching him *travel* somewhere?

We could say that Walker seeks Chris because he felt bereft at the Curson Terrace residence, and he wants comfort. Once he reaches Chris's apartment – which the Organisation has trashed – we sense a softness we've not seen before. As he stares into a shattered mirror – a sign of his fractured self, yes, but also of a plurality of possibilities – Chris appears, and he says, empathetically, 'They really got to you, huh?' She tosses the envelope containing the $1,000 to the floor and bitterly says she got well paid for fingering Mal. Rather than getting defensive, Walker picks up a bent trumpet, and speaks once more, gently: 'The guy you were going around with, spent some time here,

The Antonioni date

huh?' Her guard now lowering, she tells him that most of the things
were his. 'What are you going to do now?' Walker asks, once more
with concern. Chris, now attuned to his vulnerability, wonders, is he
asking her on a date? As Walker stands there sheepishly, she giggles.[74]

Theirs is a date Antonioni might have planned. The two sit across
from each other in a garish coffee shop, mostly deserted. It is futuristic
– there's a Googie vibe – with huge windows for walls and shiny white
tables and sky-blue benches. Chris has traded her yellow dress for a
bright orange one; Walker still wears the greenish suit he donned on
his last visit to Carter. Chris silently eats, and she drinks her soda from
a straw. She grins at Walker. Coffee only in front of him, Walker also
doesn't speak, but he is awkward, a clumsy high schooler.

In fewer than twenty-four hours, Walker has progressed from
demeaning Chris to courting her. Perhaps he is weary of the violence
and starting to realise that the $93,000 will not make him whole.
Maybe a romance with Chris will.

* * *

Not so. Walker's trauma still reigns.

See Chris in a medium shot. She stands outside in the dark,
behind a glass door. The metal framing on either side of the door
intensifies her presence. She shines like a work of art. To the left of

the door, far in the foreground and looking large, is a stone statue of a nude woman, classical in style. Chris calls, 'Walker?' Like a piece of ancient art, the moment is archetypal, one person not just hailing another but inquiring, 'Who are you?' For this scene to arise at this juncture is apt: Walker seems to be in a transition from cold criminal to awkward lover.

The next event reinforces this idea: the isolated Walker moves towards Chris. Lights flash on. Walker has turned them on from the inside and now he walks towards us. But Boorman has made no cut. We have been watching Chris watch herself in her reflection in the door. We have not been on the outside looking in, but on the outside looking at the outside. Chris has truly been, like an artwork, an image. In this case, her looking at her mirror self isn't narcissistic but introspective. In calling for the identity of Walker, she is also wondering about her own. She is the opposite of her narcissistic sister.

Stepping towards Chris, Walker, his face lighted, appears to the left of the metal doorframe, while Chris remains to the right, in the darkness. They inhabit different worlds. But Walker unlocks the door – just as Chris did for him so he could get into Mal's room – and welcomes her inside. Chris enters, and the two are together.

But this isn't a moment of union. The instant Chris finds herself in Brewster's home, Walker reverts to his brusque detachment. As he goes around closing all the blinds – not to create an intimate environment but to prepare for Brewster – he explains the situation to Chris. This house is Brewster's, it is owned by the Organisation, it's used for meetings. Chris wants to know why she is there. 'You're safer with me,' Walker replies. But what if Brewster comes? He will, and soon. And when he does, Chris says facetiously, 'And you'll ask [Brewster] for your money, he'll say no, and you'll kill him.' With equal sarcasm, Walker counters, 'Something like that.' And then, cruelly, 'What did you think this was, a pitch?' Meaning: did you think I brought you here to seduce you?

Chris is sick of Walker's inconsistency. She slaps at him with her left hand; he blocks it. 'Forget it,' he snarls.

Living art; on the verge of union; separate ways

Man of stone

She tries to clock him with the purse in her right hand. Again, he deflects. 'You forget it!' she yells, and then she wails on him, throwing blows from right and left.

Walker easily blocks the blows at first, but then just stands there and takes it – a slap to the face, a purse to the shoulder. Chris drops her purse and goes crazy on him, slapping his chest with both hands, over and over. Walker doesn't budge. Chris exhausts herself, falls down. Walker adjusts his tie and walks away.

This scene is mostly comical, a satire of a couple from a 1950s domestic sitcom having a spat. (Think *I Love Lucy* [CBS, 1951–7] and *The Donna Reed Show* [ABC, 1958–66]).[75] But the episode is also a sad allegory of blood versus stone. The animated Chris is desperate for Walker to show her affection. But here, granite-like, he won't. Like a lovelorn sprite, Chris transforms herself into a barrage of hammers. She will break through the rock, to the heart. Walker stands adamantine.

With Chris still on the floor, Walker moves into the living room, sits on the couch, turns on the TV with the remote, and flips to a film, *The Cobweb* (1955), directed by Vincente Minnelli. A young man – John Kerr – talks to Lauren Bacall, on staff at the psychiatric institution where the film is set. Kerr's Steven, a patient, wonders if his interaction with her might 'get me over my neurotic inertia'. Walker flips to a show playing military march music. Then to another, an ad for Pond's cold cream, in which a woman (an uncredited Barbara Feldon) says she creams 'twice for a night each week with Pond's cold cream', and this keeps her looking young.

This is a further satire of the 'man-of-the-house' of the 1950s suburban sitcom. Walker distracts himself from strong and perhaps unsettling feelings – of affection, of anger – by watching TV. He's had a hard day of working, after all, and deserves to escape into a world where nervous paralysis can be overcome, the army is triumphant, a woman can 'cream' every night. But the irony is sad: Walker himself is neurotically inert, his violence has been ineffective, and he ignores a young woman sexually ready for him.

While Walker disregards Chris, she struggles up and exits the living room. A din of machines comes from the kitchen. Walker checks it out. Chris has turned on every appliance: the toaster, two blenders, the mixer. The water also runs, and the dishwasher and refrigerator are open. A flustered Walker shuts it all down.

Chris is having her own satire. Unlike Walker, though, she is aware of her mockery. Where Walker exaggerates the habits of a stereotypical 1950s corporate male, Chris distorts the domestic behaviours of the idealised mid-century suburban housewife – in the kitchen, enjoying the most recent gadgets. (Though Chris in her disruptive behaviour is far closer to Lucille Ball's slapsticky Lucy than to Donna Reed's milder Donna Stone.)

Chris isn't finished. Just after a flustered Walker deals with the kitchen, upbeat jazz blasts through the house. A worked-up Walker moves from room to room seeking the power switch. Along the way, he comes across Chris dancing with a highball glass in her hand – again sending up typical upper-middle-class consumers.

Walker finally kills the music, only to find that Chris has ignited all the lights of the pool. While he's turning them off, she speaks on the intercom. The satire has ended. She speaks the truth directly:

You're a pathetic sight, Walker, from where I'm standing. You're chasing shadows, played out. It's over, finished. What would you do with the money if you got it? Wasn't yours in the first place. Why don't you just lie down, and die?

The house has revealed the most unattractive, clichéd part of Walker's identity: the money-hungry criminal who secretly desires what his enemy has – power, comfort and status. To Chris, who has just as much reason to hate the Organisation as Walker, this ache is pathetic.

Once more, an irritated Walker storms through the house in search of a switch. He bursts into a games room, and there is Chris. She pretends to play pool. Again trying to reclaim Walker, to return him to that vulnerable playfulness that promises affection, she … whacks him on the head with the thick end of her cue. The tough guy staggers back, lunges weakly at Chris. She dodges him. He lunges again, falls, but this time tackles her by the feet. She goes down, too, finds herself on her back, Walker now on top. They relax. They kiss.

The next sequence, much imitated,[76] is a tour de force of editing. The instant Walker and Chris touch lips, they are no longer on the floor of a poolroom; they are in a bed, unclothed, Walker on top of Chris, their faces in close-up, shot from Walker's left side. They slowly roll to his left, towards us. As they complete their turn, Chris has morphed into Lynne. Now Lynne and Walker roll towards us, and Walker turns into Mal. Another turn, and Chris is on top of Mal. Another roll, and we are back in the poolroom where Chris and Walker are clothed, but Chris is now on top of Walker. They are kissing. Cut to Chris lying on her back in bed, Walker lying beside her, his left arm over her chest. Chris has her left arm draped under his. She is grinning. They have made love. The camera glides towards

Chris and Walker

Lynne and Walker

Lynne and Mal

Chris and Mal

them, then shifts to a close-up showing the bottom halves of their faces, Walker's shoulder and Chris's hand. She holds him tight. Then Walker is on his back, Chris's head on his chest. We can see a scar just left of Walker's navel: where Mal shot him.

In whacking Walker, Chris challenged his masculinity. She made him vulnerable – where she wants him to be. The result of her violence is gentle: the two characters kiss. *Finally*, we think, they will express their love and be together, and Walker will let go of his quest. But then his trauma pulls him backward. While he kisses Chris, she becomes Lynne: all women are versions of his dead wife, double-crossers. Worse, kissing Lynne, he becomes Mal. Any erotic moment is infected with betrayal – regret over past betrayals, fear of new ones. Moreover, in taking his wife and money, Mal occupies a space Walker properly should occupy, and so Walker fantasises about becoming his enemy. Then Lynne becomes Chris and there is Mal yet again taking Walker's place, stealing his woman. But just when it appears that Walker's trauma is consuming him again, there he is on the poolroom floor with Chris, and she is on top – again placing him in the more vulnerable position – and they kiss, and then they are in bed together, in the afterglow of lovemaking. There is hope.

But there is the scar. Chris caresses this mark of Walker's wound, and the opening scene of the film flashes onto the screen: a gunshot, and Walker falling back into the prison cell. Chris's touch has activated in Walker a traumatic dream. And this painful repetition separates the lovers. In the next shot, Walker faces away from Chris. He is awake. He sits up, reaches under his pillow. Nothing there. He searches under Chris's pillow, and there it is: his revolver, his true love.

Gun in hand, Walker leaves the bedroom. He's wary; Brewster might have arrived. He pulls open the curtain to look outside. Flash to his pulling back the curtain in Lynne's apartment after discovering she's dead. He returns to the bedroom, and he places his hand on Chris's bare arm, preparing to shake her. But she opens her eyes, smiles. Flash to his mustering her sleeping form, pills beside her, back in her apartment, a repeat of his trying to rouse Lynne from her overdose.

11 Dissolution

Boorman rips us away from the Brewster house and Walker's
possibilities. An airstrip, obstreperous engines, garish sun. Brewster
has arrived. From the minute we encounter him, we are thankful.
After all of Walker's brooding, Mal's anxiety and Carter's blandness,
Carroll O'Connor flaunts like Falstaff. He's seen it all, and it's all
ridiculous, so why not make some dough and have a laugh? Beside
this bombastic crime boss, Walker appears dour and small.

Brewster struts off his chartered plane. Carter's hitman is
there, says he's not been paid for killing Stegman. The man who was
supposed to pay him, Carter, is dead. When the hitman asks Brewster
if he's upset over the death of his colleague, Brewster smiles big,
exclaims 'I love it.' Then, barely stifling a laugh, he adds, 'That leaves
you in a spot, though. You killed the man that's supposed to pay you.'
When the shooter protests, Brewster looks at the propeller just firing
up, spreads his hands into a 'what can I do?' pose, smiles big again,
and yells, 'I can't hear you!' When the hitman says Fairfax will get
him his money, Brewster, pleased with his wit, says, 'And if he doesn't,
maybe you can kill him, too!'

Comic relief

Walker waits for Brewster. He wears an orange shirt – matching Chris's orange dress – and a copper coat. But's he's no longer with Chris emotionally. He looks at the empty bed and flashes to his wife lying dead. When Chris emerges from the bathroom wearing all white – the life's gone out of her – Walker ignores her, starts out of the room. Then Chris asks if Walker knows her last name. He retorts: 'Do you know my first?' Neither knows the answer. They are strangers.

Brewster arrives. Walker knocks out his bodyguard. (Doing so, he flashes back to hitting Stegman's goons in The Movie House.) The instant Brewster realises he's now alone with a man who's likely to kill him, he doesn't express fear, like Mal, or bafflement, like Carter. He turns on Walker in faux anger, points at him, yells the obvious so

intensely that even Walker finds it a little funny: 'You're a very bad
man, Walker, a very destructive man. Why do you go around doing
things like this? [He points to his unconscious bodyguard.] Whadda
you want?'

Walker is on his heels. Brewster has made him feel a little
absurd. In a weak, hesitant voice, he replies, 'I want my money. I want
my 93 grand.' (He flits to the moment he asked a terrified Mal for the
dough.) Brewster can't believe it – a man threatening a huge financial
structure like the Organisation for only $93,000. Surely he wants
something else. No, Walker claims, almost mumbling. 'I ... I ... really
want my money.' (Jump to his demanding his money from Carter.)
'I'm not going to give you money,' Brewster bellows. 'Nobody is!'
(Flash again: Walker discovers the fake money in the storm drain,
Walker fires into his wife's empty bed.) But surely someone can.
Walker asks feebly, 'Who ... who runs things?'

A mark of Walker's weakness is the rapidity of his traumatic
flashbacks. Every sentence yanks him back to a similar moment from
his past, all of which are permutations of the great betrayal. It's as
though Walker, after putting his heart briefly at risk with Chris, is
perversely and hysterically returning to what he knows best, to his
most stable identity, even if it is a self-destructive, wounded man.

Brewster answers Walker's question: 'I run things. Fairfax
just signs the cheques.' 'Call Fairfax, then,' Walker requests, almost
humbly, as he sits on a couch. (The scene takes place in Brewster's
office.) Brewster will do it, even though 'it's a total waste of time'. He
is the frustrated parent to Walker's ignorant child, playing along with
what the child wants just to show the child he's wrong. As Brewster
prepares to make the call, he reaches into a desk drawer. Suspecting
Walker might believe he's going for a gun, he produces his cigar
slowly. He smiles at Walker like Walker is an idiot.

O'Connor controls the scene. Jacobs, who recognised
O'Connor's strength and intelligence, feared this would happen.[77]
And O'Connor's Brewster reveals through his sarcasm what Chris
showed through her affection: when Walker obsessively pursues the

money, he is kind of a blockhead, a typical male who assumes that money will make him whole.

After viewing the footage of this scene, Boorman acknowledged Jacobs's concern and reshot the second part in the hope of energising his lead. As Brewster is dialling Fairfax, we witness an altered Walker. He sits on the couch, and his confusion is gone, and here is the stolid warrior, relaxed but hyper-alert, ready to pounce.

He listens to Fairfax on the speaker phone. The man corroborates Brewster. The corporation will not pay. All the while, Brewster continues his shenanigans, aping to Walker the gestures of 'I told you so.' 'How much is Brewster worth to you?' Walker asks Fairfax. When Fairfax claims he's not impressed by threatening phone calls, Walker lunges towards Brewster and *shoots the phone.*

This rage terrifies Brewster. He quickly loses his wise-assing gumption. Chris appears from another room. She wears a red coat

Shooting the phone

Walker yet again broods over Alcatraz

over her white dress. This is Mal's colour. Minus Walker, will she slide into the sleazy world of crime and seduction?

Walker is now in charge. With no aplomb, Brewster offers Walker an opportunity to get the cash. He can accompany Brewster to the old Alcatraz run, the last Organisation drop involving large amounts of cash. The location is different – Fort Point – but everything else is the same. The deadpan Walker stares straight ahead, ominously says, 'Alcatraz.' The camera moves in, an extreme close-up, the only such shot of Walker in the entire film. We are now entering his deepest interiors, his reckoning.

* * *

Walker strides in the dark, wearing the same orange suit, carrying his .44. He is on a rectangular tier some fifty feet above an open courtyard. A third tier rises above. Below, in the centre of the courtyard, is Brewster. He directs Walker to a light switch. When the switch ignites, a spotlight hits Brewster. Chris is nowhere to be seen.

This is Fort Point, which rests at the base of the southern side of Golden Gate Bridge. Completed for the Civil War but never used, this 'Third System' fort of brick-and-mortar levels and arches feels more like a Piranesi prison than a bastion of security, and Boorman makes full use of its labyrinthine circuits and chiaroscuro lighting.

Fort Point

As Walker glides through the shadows, Brewster reassures him that everything is on the up-and-up, he will finally get his dough. No longer the wise-cracking alpha, Brewster is the butt of a joke he can't understand. Shot from above – from Walker's vantage – he looks like a clown doing a nervous schtick for an audience of one.

What Brewster is to this drop – isolated, unsure, powerless – Walker was to the one in Alcatraz. Now Walker appears to be in the ascendant, in Mal's position. But he might not be. That's why he walks the corridors, searching for treachery.

A helicopter nears. Walker descends to Brewster's ground level. He asks about Fairfax. What's his role in all this? Brewster tells him

More shadows

that Fairfax is either dead or soon will be. Walker once more fades into the shadows. When the helicopter lands, Brewster makes the exchange.

Cut to Walker in close-up. Shadows form bars on his face. Only his eyes are visible. We remember similar lighting on his face as he lay wounded in Alcatraz. Is he on the verge of repeating his trauma, or will this be repetition with a difference?

The instant Brewster yells for Walker to come down for his money, Brewster gets shot in the gut. He thinks Walker did it. Yost appears from the shadows, walks casually over to the dying Brewster. 'Walker didn't shoot you,' he announces, 'I did.' Brewster strains to look up, and what he reveals conjures an alternate *Point Blank*, shocking, that has run concurrently with the one we have embraced.

Brewster calls Yost, Walker's strange guide, *Fairfax*. All along, Walker has been a pawn in Fairfax's power game. Walker's ostensible quest for wholeness, for self-understanding, for affection, has really been a directive from a mob boss: kill anyone threatening my ascendancy. In struggling to transcend the mechanics of trauma, Walker has locked himself more tightly in the cruel corporate machine. In doing away with Stegman, Mal and Carter, he has become an employee of the Organisation himself, a more lethal version of these lesser hoods.

If we feel like we do at the end of *Fight Club* (1999) or *The Usual Suspects* (1995), we should. In each of these films, we are placed in sympathy with a character bent on the truth. We want him to find what he's looking for, and we respect his insight and tenacity. But at the movie's end, we realise that our hero has been blind all along, he has been duped, and so have we. We must now accommodate a counter-narrative, one that undercuts our hard-won conclusions. The effect is uncanny. All along we've seen a movie about Walker destroying the Organisation for his own benefit. Now we witness a story about the Organisation crushing Walker for its own advantage. But the first movie remains. It is erased and sustained, just as the second picture is and is not.

As viewers, we can be dazzled by Boorman's arty legerdemain, his mercurial irony, and we can contemplate the rhetoric of vertiginous duplicity. But if we are Walker, if we are *in* the narrative, we must ask: who am I? and we must mean it, because our personal history is the reverse of what we thought.

From above, Walker watches Brewster die. Fairfax tells Walker that the deal's done. Brewster was the last one threatening to oust him from the head of the Organisation. Fairfax wants Walker to join him. He's been searching for a man like him.

Walker remains silent among the shadows, his face covered in darkness, save his eyes. He now knows that he's been the patsy all along, but he betrays no emotion, though we would expect anger and sadness. And he does not act, other than simply to vanish into the shadows. Again, we would predict the opposite. The money he's been seeking is now available; he can go get it.

But maybe he doesn't trust Fairfax. Maybe the parcel Brewster received from the helicopter is filled with paper. Maybe Fairfax has his sniper at the ready.

Well, if Walker doesn't trust Fairfax, why not take him out? The man has manipulated him, and he is the boss of the Organisation that crushed his spirit and Chris's. Walker's got his .44.

Why does Walker stay in the dark? Aside from practical reasons – avoiding another plot of Fairfax – he might vanish because he's seen himself clearly for the first time, and he loathes what he sees. Far from a man questing to recover from his humanity, he's a cog in a criminal machine.[78]

But there's another possible reason for his fade. Now aware of the harrowing consequences of his misguided quest, he chooses to eschew a definite identity altogether, to ease into a state of potentiality from which he might emerge a new man.[79]

Just as we hover between contradictory *Point Blank* narratives, we also find ourselves between two equally valid accounts of Walker's odd retreat: the suicide theory and the liberation vision. It's like balancing at the end of Truffaut's *Les Quatre cents coups/*

The 400 Blows (1959): as Antoine (Jean-Pierre Léaud) stands before
the ocean, he is both desolate *and* liberated. The ambiguity can be
paralysing; it can be liberating. It is usually both.

The hitman appears beside Fairfax. It was he who killed
Brewster. Was the plan for him to shoot Walker, too? Probably.

Walker backs further into the darkness. Boorman holds the
camera on the blackness his protagonist has become. The shooter
starts to pick up the money. Leave it, orders Fairfax. The two men
exit the fort.

Cut to an aerial shot of Brewster lying dead in the centre of
the courtyard. Music eerily similar to that which began the movie,
sounds. The camera raises above the ramparts and then directs
towards San Francisco, before gliding to Alcatraz, where the film
began. The final credits roll. The prison rises in the background.

From whose point of view do we see these things? We don't
know, but here is one possibility: this is Walker's perspective. He
has faded into the air, and in doing so, he has shed his old identity
as Fairfax's tool, and his body too, and now he can float about
unhindered. His first long gaze is aptly on Alcatraz. He is no longer
immured there. The many bars that have fallen across him have
vanished, and he moves about like a spirit.[80]

But one could suppose with equal validity that the hovering
camera expresses not Walker's vision but the perspective of the

Who sees Alcatraz?

director, Boorman, glad to leave behind this sordid world he has created, a vast prison. In this interpretation, Walker remains in Piranesian Fort Point and so ends where he began: betrayed (by Yost), wounded (psychologically) and entrapped. The only animating force in his life, Chris, has disappeared.

If Boorman in the end resembles a demiurge abandoning his terrifying creation, do we, the audience, want to transcend Walker's purgatory as well? Certainly the expectations we brought to a Hollywood crime thriller have been dashed, and we are left with insoluble mysteries. Are we glad to be done with *Point Blank*?

No, is the probable answer, and this is the brilliance of Boorman's film. Though the content is painful, the form exhilarates, and so does the acting. We watch the picture again and again, just as we repeatedly ride the same roller coaster (though it might twist our stomachs) or drink the same gin (despite the hangover). Like the films of Truffaut and Resnais and Godard, and more recently like the pictures of Spike Lee, Quentin Tarantino and Jane Campion, *Point Blank*'s style imbues its grim matter with an addictive gusto.

12 Sex and Sadism

MGM was down on *Point Blank* throughout its shooting and would
have pulled the plug if it weren't for Marvin. Boorman's finished
product did nothing to raise the studio's spirits. The executives forced
him to show his cut to the formidable Margaret Booth, who had been
with the studio since the 1920s and had edited for Louis B. Mayer
himself. Her credits included *Mutiny on the Bounty* (1935), *Camille*
(1936) and *A Yank at Oxford* (1938), and she would go on to edit *The
Way We Were* (1973), *The Goodbye Girl* (1977) and *Annie* (1982).
But her role at MGM extended beyond her individual credits. As the
studio's supervising film editor, she weighed in on every film the studio
made, and her authority was considerable. Surely, MGM thought,
this legendary personage, with very traditional taste, would impel this
inexperienced director to get his film into a more marketable shape?

This did not happen. After she and Boorman watched the cut
together – she wore slippers and warmed her feet with a small heater
– she had only minor suggestions. Boorman incorporated them, and
Booth screened the slightly revised version for the executives. They
were, to use Boorman's word, 'baffled'. When the film ended, they
immediately started murmuring about edits and reshoots. But before
anyone found a voice, Booth, from the back of the room, boomed,
'You change one frame of this movie over my dead body.'[81]

And so the film would stay almost exactly as Boorman wanted
it. How, then, to market this strange, seemingly doomed-to-flop film?
Sell its sex and violence. MGM's advertising campaign focused so
pantingly on skin and blood that *Point Blank* in the publicity ended
up looking more like a drive-in exploitation than a slick Hollywood
thriller, much less an ardent probing of trauma.

Though a theatrical release poster benefits from a simple,
elegant Saul-Bass-like, mid-century modern design – the background

is white with a bright yellow border and a vivid red square in the middle – it is crude pulp. Marvin is large just left of the centre, his .44 hanging phallically near his crotch. Behind him is a composite of six scenes: Acker lying on her back in a tight miniskirt, breasts pert; Marvin and Dickinson in a bed nude; Marvin with his hand around a falling Acker's neck, his gun out; Marvin pulling a man down from behind; Marvin firing his gun to the right of the picture; Marvin again with his hand around Acker's neck as she hits the ground, his gun at the ready. Of these scenes, one doesn't exist in the film (Acker lying on her back in sexual readiness), and two (Marvin choking Acker) are from the same moment. Clearly the studio wants to emphasise not only sex and violence separately, but sex and violence combined: sadistic eroticism. The text to the left of Walker's pistol says it all: 'There are two kinds of people in his up-tight world: his victims and his women. And sometimes you can't tell them apart.'

'Up-tight world'

That the recognisable Marvin is front and centre shows that
MGM is trying to capitalise on his star power, but the sex and violence
overwhelm the poster. This is true of the other publicity posters. A
theatrical release one-sheet depicts a concentric blue target in the
background, with Marvin's gun large and jutting phallically from the
page. The barrel is right in the bull's-eye of the target. To the left of the
gun's butt is Marvin's face. At the bottom of the poster, just right of
centre, is a small black-and-white image of Dickinson. It is hard to tell
if she is erotically sprawled or knocked down. The same text about sex
and violence in this 'up-tight world' is positioned below the target.

Point Blank's pressbook features these images. In addition, it
contains an article highlighting Marvin's sexuality, gawking at his

Bull's-eye
(LMPC/Getty Images)

'Hemingwayesque' penchant for 'lusty living'. He enjoys 'plenty of action' around his Malibu home, and he parties down in Culver City's 'only topless nightery'.[82] An article on Dickinson states that her relationship with Marvin in the film is 'a violent one, both physically and emotionally'.[83] Boorman's is the only presence in the kit who intimates the film's emotional power, which springs from Marvin's feminine sensitivity.

Magazine and newspaper advertisements also emphasise sex and violence. A *Daily News* ad of September of 1967 quotes reviewer Kathleen Carroll: *Point Blank* is a 'STUDY IN SEX AND SADISM!' The other quotes in the ad emphasise the same theme. '"Point Blank" comes to the screen in "a blaze of gunfire and colour"' (*New York Times*); it is '[t]hreatening and violent' (*New York Post*); 'it hits like a fat slug from the .38 [*sic*]' (*Newsweek*); it is a 'nightmare … [with] a hovering sense of menace' (*Saturday Review*).

The official trailer likewise pushes sadistic sex. It opens with Marvin bursting through Acker's door, throwing her down, firing into her bed. The music sounds like a cavalry charge, eons away from Mandel's eerie score. Cut to Walker stomping down the corridor, while a dead-serious voiceover says that Walker is an 'emotional and primitive man' – patently untrue. With Walker's footsteps in the background, the trailer cuts to Mal unbuttoning Chris's dress, to a voiceover of Chris saying of Walker what she really says of Mal, that he makes her flesh crawl. Right after this misattribution, we see Walker and Chris fall to the floor at Brewster's, only the scene looks like Walker is sexually assaulting Chris. A montage of Walker roughing up his enemies follows (the corridor steps still clomping), and then the trailer shifts to Mal shooting the drop men in Alcatraz; only the preview makes it look like Walker is doing the shooting.

* * *

Point Blank enjoyed mostly positive reviews upon its release in New York's DeMille and Coronet theatres on 19 September 1967. (It had premiered three weeks earlier in San Francisco's Paramount Theatre.)

Tellingly, the earliest reviews praised the film's successful rendering of its more traditional genre elements. Bosley Crowther of the *New York Times* found *Point Blank* to be 'candid and calculatedly sadistic'.[84] A young Roger Ebert gave the picture three out of four stars in the *Chicago Sun-Times*; he found *Point Blank*, as 'suspense thrillers' go, 'pretty good', and he liked Marvin as 'a plain, simple tough guy'.[85] In the *Washington Post*, Sam Lesner liked the movie for its 'lightning action' (though he wasn't wild about its 'confounding stream-of-consciousness' style).[86] John L. Wasserman of the *San Francisco Chronicle* praised Boorman for his 'chillingly effective' 'scenes of violence and brutality'.[87] Other periodicals praising the film's pulpier elements were the *New York Daily News*, the *New York Post, Newsweek* and the *Saturday Review*.

Some of the less positive reviews – there are a handful – point to parts of the film that go beyond genre. In *Film Quarterly*, Dan Bates speculated that audiences would not care for Boorman's 'peculiarly sardonic view', even if it 'adds up to something more enlightening than the viewer drawn out for some blazing movie action is likely to expect'.[88] Manny Farber in *Artforum* emphasises the film's tension between genre and avant-garde. If the picture's 'tough ad' leads you to expect hard-boiled action, the film itself is a 'fantasy' about a 'strangely unhealthy tactility. All physical matter seems to be coated.'[89] Farber laments that Boorman's visuals reduce humans to machines.

But what Farber views as flaw, Boorman embraces as virtue: an exploration of the dehumanising forces of the modern world. Writers with the advantage of temporal distance – roughly a year – recognised this quality of Boorman's film. Stephen Farber in his *Sight and Sound* essay of 1968 places *Point Blank* in a distinguished group of 'outlaw' films, including *Bonnie and Clyde* (1967), that challenge 'socially accepted distinctions of sanity and morality' and locate value on the 'outsider'.[90] Also in '68, James Michael Martin in *Film Quarterly* praises the film's epistemological elements, focusing on how Walker's subjective 'reality … is a curious blend of natural phenomena and

POINT BLANK | 99

mental associations, déjà vu and recapitulation'.[91] In a 1969 piece in
Sight and Sound, John Lindsay Brown calls *Point Blank* one of the key
films of the past decade in its 'expression of the spirit of frustration
in the face of totalitarian society and of subsequent, compensatory
violence, a spirit that unifies Dallas, Detroit and Berkeley'.[92]

Point Blank's box-office performance was respectable. Its 1967
gross of about $9 million[93] (the film ultimately cost $2.5 million to
make) put it among the top thirty earners of the year.[94] Released
within months of *The Dirty Dozen*, *Point Blank* was basically
competing against itself, with both pictures featuring Lee Marvin as
the anti-hero. Directed by the distinguished Robert Aldrich, acted by
a formidable ensemble (including Ernest Borgnine, Charles Bronson,
John Cassavetes and Jim Brown), and depicting an ever-popular
subject matter (World War II), *The Dirty Dozen* was bound to win out.

In fact, 1967 wasn't only the year Aldrich's Marvin beat out
Boorman's; it was also the year that several other scofflaw anti-heroes
out-earned Walker. The most prominent example of this was Warren
Beatty's Clyde. The film featuring this American bank robber was
released only weeks before *Point Blank*, and it became a sensation.
Audiences had never seen such extreme violence in a Hollywood
film; nor had they witnessed such a striking blend of American genre
conventions and New Wave techniques. By the time *Point Blank*
came out, *Bonnie and Clyde* had taken up the massive cultural space
Boorman's film might have filled.

But even if *Bonnie and Clyde* had not distracted audiences from
Point Blank, the film still might not have been a top grosser. After all,
even though *Point Blank* shares qualities with Beatty's picture, it is,
by the standards of 1960s' Hollywood cinema, very strange. Marvin
might be an anti-hero like Beatty, but where Beatty aims to endear
himself to audiences, Marvin doesn't fear alienating viewers. Ever
since *The Wild One* (1953), *The Big Heat*, *Bad Day at Black Rock*
(1955) and *The Man Who Shot Liberty Valance* (1962), he had been
playing unsympathetic characters. But at least the characters in these
films are recognisably evil and so ultimately reassuring, fitting within a

familiar dualistic framework. You know who they are, and you know how they can be stopped. In *Point Blank*, though, Marvin is frequently … *blank*. US audiences weren't used to this kind of ambiguity. And then there's the film's experimental form. Where *Bonnie and Clyde*'s New Wave elements are dynamic and playful (inspired by the Truffaut of *Jules et Jim* [1962]), the European aspects of *Point Blank* indicate stasis and alienation – the mnemonic repetitions of Resnais, Antonioni's empty cities. *Point Blank*'s sexuality is disconcerting, too. Bonnie and Clyde might have trouble consummating their union sexually but in the end the film asserts traditional romanticism: the intensity of their love is consummated in their early deaths, à la Romeo and Juliet. Walker and Chris drift in the barren worlds of Pinter and Beckett. They might be capable of having sex, but Walker appears indifferent before and after, and Chris is confused.

Point Blank was celebrated by French critics after its opening in their country in April of 1968. For about twenty years after, the film gained cult status, more likely to be spoken in the same breath as *The Naked Kiss* (1964) or *El Topo* (1970) than *Touch of Evil* or *Hiroshima mon amour*. In a 1987 piece in *Film Comment* listing his 'guilty' pleasures, Brian De Palma made the connection between Boorman's film and the aforementioned ones of Sam Fuller and Alejandro Jodorowsky; he appreciated in these 'offbeat movies' an exploration of 'intense psychological traumas'.[95] In 1988, when *Point Blank* was released on VHS, critics began to pronounce the film a classic.

By 1998, *Point Blank*'s reputation had grown to the point that the movie was re-released in theatres. David Thomson expressed a particular obsession with the film in *Sight and Sound*. Though he was troubled by some of the picture's irreducible ambiguities, he concluded that *Point Blank* was 'the first and maybe still the richest merging of an American genre with European arthouse aspirations'.[96] Elsewhere, he hailed the film as a 'masterpiece'.[97]

A primary reason for *Point Blank*'s revival was that the movies it had influenced were creating an audience for it that simply didn't exist in the 1960s. According to Tarantino, *Point Blank* significantly shaped *Reservoir Dogs* (1992),[98] and it's hard to imagine Michael Mann fashioning his desolate LA cityscapes in *Heat* (1995) without Boorman somewhere in his mind.[99] But take away these films, and perhaps *Point Blank* would not have enjoyed such a successful re-release.

Soon after its reappearance in theatres, other significant films deliberately modelled themselves on *Point Blank*, further enhancing its reputation. Steven Soderbergh's *The Limey* (1999) is essentially a remake of the film, as is Christopher Nolan's *Memento* (2000). Jim Jarmusch has admitted that *Point Blank* shaped his vision for *The Limits of Control* (2009).[100] And Nicolas Winding Refn has likened his relationship to Ryan Gosling, star of his gritty LA crime film *Drive* (2011), to the partnership between Boorman and Marvin in *Point Blank*.[101]

Point Blank was released on Blu-ray in 2005 – the extras include commentary by Soderbergh and Boorman – and in 2013 was again released in theatres. The BFI staged a retrospective of Boorman's work in 2014, and *Point Blank* was a prominent part of the celebration. Walker's LAX shoes were on display.

* * *

From Bloomington to London the shoes travelled, and still, in every showing of *Point Blank*, they hammer the earth. They mark the relentlessness the film so indelibly pounds home – the relentlessness of pain and grace's perseverance. That the torment and the mercy need one another to exist but also remain blind to each other's presence is one of the film's most profound and troubling revelations. Marvin's anguished tenderness and Boorman's dazzling fractures embody this vexed paradox of unity and brokenness, as do some of the blackest comedies of our time, and the most ecstatic tragedies.

Notes

1 John Boorman, *Adventures of a Suburban Boy* (London: Faber and Faber, 2003), p. 109.
2 Pauline Kael, *5001 Nights at the Movies* (New York: Picador, 1991), p. 321.
3 Ibid.
4 Boorman, *Adventures*, p. 118.
5 Ibid., pp. 120–1, 126.
6 Ibid., p. 126. In *The Cinema of John Boorman* (Lanham, MD: Scarecrow Press, 2012), pp. 28–9, Brian Hoyle reminds us that another factor in Hollywood's sudden interest in 'arty' European directors such as Boorman was the recent failure of big-budget films such as *Cleopatra* (1963) and *Doctor Dolittle* (1967). Studios had hoped that such spectacles would draw growing television audiences back into theatres. By the late 1960s, this plan was clearly not working, so studios started developing smaller films with more aesthetic integrity. This shift bred of financial necessity was a major factor in the birth of the so-called 'New Hollywood'.
7 Boorman, *Adventures*, p. 126.
8 Ibid., p. 127.
9 Ibid. In *Detours and Lost Highways: A Map of Neo-Noir* (New York: Limelight, 1999), p. 166, Foster Hirsch calls Walker a 'pit of male anxiety'. Mark Harris notes that Westlake himself imagined Parker (Boorman's Walker) as Jack Palance, who certainly shares with Marvin a face of melancholy granite ('Cinema '67 Revisited: Point Blank', *Film Comment* 30 August 2017. Available at: <https://www.filmcomment.com/blog/cinema-67-revisited-point-blank/> [accessed 18 July 2022]).

10 Dwayne Epstein, *Lee Marvin: Point Blank* (Tucson, AZ: Schaffner Press, 2013), pp. 48–52.
11 Boorman, 'My Difficult Friend', *Irish Times*, 13 June 1998. Available at: <https://www.irishtimes.com/news/my-difficult-friend-1.162944> (accessed 7 July 2022).
12 Boorman, *Adventures*, p. 127.
13 Ibid., p. 128.
14 Ibid.
15 Ibid.
16 Boorman, interviewed by Michel Ciment, *John Boorman*, trans. Gilbert Adair (London: Faber and Faber, 1986), p. 76.
17 Alexander Jacobs, interviewed by Stephen Farber, 'The Writer II: An Interview with Alexander Jacobs', *Film Quarterly* 22:2 (Winter 1968–9), p. 5.
18 Boorman, interviewed by Michel Ciment, p. 76.
19 Boorman mentions *Point Blank*'s structural affinities with Resnais in his interview with Michel Ciment, p. 76. In his *Adventures*, he notes Pinter's influence on dialogue, p. 129. On that page he also claims that *Point Blank*'s 'fractured' form was influenced by Jean Renoir. This must be a typo, since Renoir is famous for the transparency of his style, for how his stories unfold clearly and naturalistically. I think Boorman intended to say here that Resnais, not Renoir, shaped his jagged narrative. Peter Cowie specifically connects *Point Blank* to *Hiroshima mon amour* in *Revolution! The Explosion of World Cinema in the 1960s* (London: Faber and Faber, 2004), pp. 229–30.

20 John Boorman, 'Notes', Boorman, John MSS, 1940–2014, Subseries *Point Blank* (1967), LMC 2889, Lilly Library, Indiana University, Bloomington.

21 Ibid.

22 Ibid.

23 Alexander Jacobs, Letter of 19 December 1966, Boorman, 'Correspondence, 1966–1969', in Boorman, John MSS, 1940–2014, Subseries *Point Blank* (1967), LMC 2889, Lilly Library, Indiana University, Bloomington.

24 Jacobs, Letter of 19 December 1966.

25 Alexander Jacobs, Letter of 20 March 1967, Boorman, 'Correspondence, 1966–1969', in Boorman, John MSS, 1940–2014, Subseries *Point Blank* (1967), LMC 2889, Lilly Library, Indiana University, Bloomington.

26 Ibid.

27 Jacobs, interviewed by Stephen Farber, pp. 6–7.

28 Walter Hill, interviewed by Patrick McGilligan, *Backstory 4: Interviews with Screenwriters of the 1970s and 1980s*, ed. Patrick McGilligan (Berkeley: University of California Press, 2006), p. 112.

29 Boorman, *Adventures*, p. 133.

30 Ibid.

31 Ibid., p. 134.

32 Ibid., p. 138.

33 Boorman, interviewed by Michel Ciment, p. 72.

34 Boorman, *Adventures*, p. 138.

35 Epstein, *Lee Marvin*, pp. 162–3.

36 Jacobs, Letter of 19 December 1966.

37 In an interview with Dwayne Epstein, Marvin's biographer, Angie Dickinson said of the actor: 'He did have a sadness about him. Sad, sad, sad. When people are sad, you want to make them not sad. For me at least, it just made me want to be better. I never analyzed it beyond that' (Dwayne Epstein, 'Exclusive: Frequent Costar Angie Dickinson on Lee Marvin', Dwayne Epstein: Author of *Lee Marvin: Point Blank*, 24 November 2014. Available at: <http://pointblankbook.com/exclusive-frequent-costar-angie-dickinson-on-lee-marvin/> [accessed 13 July 2022]).

38 Howard Hampton, 'Face Off: Howard Hampton on *Red River* and *Point Blank*', *Artforum*, 18 July 2014. Available at: <https://www.artforum.com/film/howard-hampton-on-red-river-and-point-blank-47418> (accessed 13 July 2022).

39 Irwin Winkler, *Life in the Movies: Stories from Fifty Years in Hollywood* (New York: Abrams, 2019), p. 21.

40 Ibid.

41 Boorman, 'Notes'.

42 Ibid.

43 Ibid.

44 Ibid.

45 John Boorman, *Point Blank*, DVD Commentary (Burbank, CA: Warner Home Video, 2014).

46 Boorman, *Adventures*, p. 129.

47 Ibid.

48 Ibid., p. 132.

49 Robert Carringer writes that 'Los Angeles is a visual correlative for Walker's rootlessness and lack of a past. It is a place dominated by massive, forbidding concrete forms … and the faceless, impassive, unornamented buildings of postwar era construction' ('Hollywood's Los Angeles: Two Paradigms', *Looking for Los Angeles:*

Architecture, Film, Photography, and the Urban Landscape, eds Charles D. Salas and Michael S. Roth [Los Angeles: Getty Research Institute, 2001], p. 258). In 'Cinema '67 Revisited', Harris celebrates the film's 'punitively grey concrete cityscape – skyscrapers, viaducts, tunnels, garages, overpasses – not to mention offices and homes where the dominant hues are industrial shades of avocado, orange, and khaki'.

50 Excellent overviews of how European directors envisioned Los Angeles in the New Hollywood are Michael S. Duffy, 'Eurovisions: Alternative Views of the Hollywood Landscape', *World Film Locations: Los Angeles*, ed. Gabriel Solomons (Bristol: Intellect Books, 2011), pp. 122–3; and Gabriel Solomons, 'Los Angeles', *Big Picture Magazine* 16 (September/October 2011), p. 26.

51 Alex Lines nicely sums up the role of Alcatraz in the film: 'The use of Alcatraz Prison is the film's first sign of its thematic depth, as contextually the audience is aware that the prison is infamous for being inescapable. … [The location] also gives a metaphorical look at the state of Walker himself – a man who has been robbed of freedom and who is stuck in the past' ('*Point Blank*: Dissecting a Forgotten Classic', *Film Inquiry*, 1 August 2016. Available at: <https://www.filminquiry.com/point-blank-retrospective/> [accessed 14 July 2022]).

52 Boorman, *Adventures*, p. 129.

53 Ibid., pp. 129–30.

54 Johnny Mandel, Liner Notes, Point Blank Soundtrack, CD, 2002, quoted in Dwayne Epstein, 'Johnny Mandel: *Point Blank*'s Composer', Dwayne Epstein: Author of *Lee Marvin: Point Blank*, 5 July 2020. Available at: <http://pointblankbook.com/johnny-mandel-point-blanks-composer/> (accessed 14 July 2022).

55 Three typical accounts of Walker as either dead for the entire film or dreaming are David Thomson, 'As I Lay Dying', *Sight and Sound* 8:6 (June 1998), pp. 14–17; Nick Schager, 'Review: *Point Blank*', *Slant*, 24 July 2003. Available at: <https://www.slantmagazine.com/film/point-blank/> (accessed 14 July 2022); and Peter Lewis, 'Is "Point Blank" a Ghost Story?', *Medium*, 21 October 2012. Available at: <https://medium.com/@plewis67/is-point-blank-a-ghost-story-c81174dc86c5> (accessed 14 July 2022).

56 Boorman, *Point Blank*, DVD Commentary. But earlier, Boorman does suggest that the film takes place entirely in Walker's head. In his interview with Michel Ciment, he says, 'Seeing the film, one should be able to imagine that this whole story of vengeance is taking place at the moment of his death' (Boorman, interviewed by Michel Ciment, p. 79).

57 Hirsch's discussion of neo-noir is excellent (pp. 1–20). He notes that *Point Blank*, one of the first neo-noir films, was 'loyal' to 'Hollywood narrative codes [while] at the same time that it slyly disrupted them' and 'established a new kind of dialogue with genre audiences' (p. 17). In his chapter on *Point Blank* as neo-noir film, Hirsch shows how the film melds tropes from classic noir (a protagonist who struggles with intimacy) and with innovations in *mise en scène* (the use of psychedelic colours) (pp. 165–9). An especially subtle take on *Point Blank* as neo-noir is Andrew Spicer's. In his essay 'Problems of Memory and Identity in Neo-Noir's Existential Anti-Hero', *The Philosophy of Neo-Noir*, ed. Mark T. Conrad (Lexington: University of Kentucky Press, 2007), Spicer shows how the film is 'an archetypal revenge thriller, but turned inside out'. Hesitation between 'mundanity and fantasy', 'realism' and 'abstraction', and 'particular' and 'universal' persistently upset the story's conventional linearity (pp. 50–3).

58 Boorman, *Point Blank*, DVD Commentary.

59 Ibid.

60 Boorman, *Adventures*, p. 136.

61 Thomson describes the courting Walker beautifully. As Walker pays 'sweet, elephantine, drunken court to' Lynne, 'he wears a brown seaman's jacket; he is with a bunch of sailors – he seems like a rogue just off a ship, salty with amorousness, his brown hair slicked down by the rain. … [H]e makes exaggerated, decorous moves on her, smiling all the while – and Lynne responds, and loosens her red-brown hair. You realise you've never seen Lee Marvin so vulnerable – was he drunk when they filmed that scene, to open up his set face?' ('As I Lay Dying', p. 14). Elsewhere, Thomson likens the courting Walker to 'a great sea creature who has come ashore to claim [Lynne]' ('A Very Bad Man', *Sight and Sound* 23:4 [April 2013], p. 38).

62 Jack Shadoian claims that '[w]hat keeps Walker from being a monster is his vulnerability'. This keeps him from being a 'pure automaton like the members of the organization'. Walker's 'sense of humor' likewise humanises him (*Dreams and Dead Ends: The American Gangster/Crime Film* [Cambridge, MA: MIT Press, 1977], p. 264).

63 Alexander Jacobs, David Newhouse and Rafe Newhouse, 'Point Blank: Original Story, Based on the Novel The Hunter, by Richard Stark', Film Script, 14 August 1967, BFI Collections, Reuben Library, SCR 14306, Reel 2, p. 3.

64 Boorman, *Point Blank*, DVD Commentary.

65 Shadoian writes that the Organisation's 'members, high and low, have no identity outside their function to the corporation' (p. 257).

66 Boorman, interviewed by Michel Ciment, p. 74. In 'A Man Out of Time: John Boorman and Lee Marvin's *Point Blank*', Adrian Danks insightfully sums up the film's take on capitalism: '*Point Blank* is a fascinating portrait of a commodified, corporate America predicated on seemingly incomprehensible financial transactions and labyrinthine chains of command. It is situated within a modern urban environment of streamlined and minimalist architecture offset by the semiotic abundance of a hyper-mediated world' (*Senses of Cinema* 45, November 2007. Available at: <https://www.sensesofcinema.com/2007/cteq/point-blank/> [accessed 20 July 2022]).

67 Of this nightclub scene, Boorman said, 'As for the nightmarish atmosphere of the discotheque, what I wanted it to express was all that violence seething inside [Walker's] head' (Boorman, interviewed by Michel Ciment, p. 74).

68 Jacobs, Newhouse, Newhouse, 'Point Blank', Reel 3, p. 3.

69 *Point Blank* Pressbook (Hollywood, CA: M-G-M, 1967), p. 2. Shadoian also notes Walker's femininity in the robe/compact scene, and he concludes that this is one of several moments in the film – including Brewster's chiding and his duping by Fairfax – that undercut Marvin's traditional 'nasty force' persona (p. 255).

70 Thomson in 'As I Lay Dying', p. 14, writes of the 'nice, resonant ping' made by Walker's breaking the lock.

71 Jacobs, Letter of 19 December 1966.

72 Thomson notes the sexual tension between Walker and Reese in 'A Very Bad Man', p. 38. Hirsch does as well (p. 166). Shadoian, too (p. 255).

73 Viktor Shklovsky, 'Art as Technique', *Modern Criticism and Theory: A Reader*, ed. David Lodge (London: Longmans, 1988), pp. 16–30. Peter Bradshaw captures *Point Blank*'s blend of familiar and strange nicely in calling it 'an angular, spiky, startling picture that shifts a knight's move away from the thriller form' ('*Point Blank* – Review', *Guardian*, 29 March 2013. Available at: <https://www.theguardian.com/film/2013/mar/28/point-blank-review> [accessed 20 July 2022]).

74 Shadoian claims that Walker 'returns to Chris's apartment for no apparent reason other than concern and perhaps companionship' (p. 264).

75 For more on gender roles in 1950s' American sitcoms, see Andrea Press's 'Gender and Family in Television's Golden Age and Beyond', *The Annals of the American Academy of Political and Social Science* 625, September 2009, pp. 139–50; and Jeanne Morreale, 'Dreams and Disruption in the Fifties Sitcom', *E-Media Studies* 4:1, 2015. Available at: <https://journals.dartmouth.edu/cgi-bin/WebObjects/Journals.woa/xmlpage/4/article/453> (accessed 7 October 2022).

76 Boorman, *Point Blank*, DVD Commentary.

77 Jacobs, Letter of 20 March 1967.

78 Schager captures Walker's potential self-loathing: 'the final image of Walker receding into the enveloping darkness is a fittingly despondent conclusion to one of noir's most bleak, vicious and inventive masterpieces'.

79 David Thomson has said that Walker at this point of the film has become 'uncontainable', 'infinite' ('Mission Intractable', *Sight and Sound* 16:2 [February 2006], p. 28).

80 Boorman in his DVD commentary on the film claims that Walker in the end 'gradually melds back into nothingness'. Shadoian agrees, observing that Walker at the end 'fades away, having accomplished nothing' (p. 257).

81 Boorman, *Adventures*, pp. 140–1.

82 *Point Blank* Pressbook, p. 2.

83 Ibid.

84 Bosley Crowther, 'Vengeful Lee Marvin in "Point Blank"', *New York Times*, 19 September 1967.

85 Roger Ebert, 'Point Blank', *Chicago Sun-Times*, 20 October 1967.

86 Sam Lesner, 'Lee Marvin's Violent World', *Washington Post*, 15 October 1967, p. L2.

87 John L. Wasserman, 'Point Blank', *San Francisco Chronicle*, 15 October 1967.

88 Dan Bates, 'Review of *Point Blank* by John Boorman', *Film Quarterly* 21:2 (Winter 1967–8), p. 63.

89 Manny Farber, '*The Train, Bonnie and Clyde, Reflections in a Golden Eye, Point Blank*', *Artforum* 6:4 (December 1967), p. 69.

90 Stephen Farber, 'The Outlaws', *Sight and Sound* 37:4 (Autumn 1968), p. 175.

91 James Michael Martin, '*Point Blank* by John Boorman, Judd Bernard', *Film Quarterly* 21:4 (Summer 1968), p. 41.

92 John Lindsay Brown, 'Islands of the Mind', *Sight and Sound* 39:1 (Winter 1969–70), p. 23.

93 Kevin Thomas, 'Chartoff and Winkler: Entrepreneurs of the Offbeat Film Two Entrepreneurs of Offbeat Movies', *Los Angeles Times*, 16 January 1968, p. D1.

94 'North America (US and Canada) Domestic Movie Chart for 1967', *The Numbers*. Available at: <https://www.the-numbers.com/market/1967/top-grossing-movies> (accessed 21 July 2022).

95 Brian De Palma, 'Guilty Pleasures: Brian De Palma', *Film Comment* 23:3 (May–June 1987), pp. 52–3.

96 Thomson, 'As I Lay Dying', p. 17.

97 David Thomson, *The New Biographical Dictionary of Film: Sixth Edition* (New York: Knopf, 2014), p. 112.

98 Amy Nicholson, 'Young Quentin Goes to the Movies: How "Point Blank" Influenced Tarantino's Directorial Debut "Reservoir Dogs"', *The Ringer*, 25 July 2019. Available at: <https://www.theringer.com/2019/7/25/20727062/quentin-tarantino-feature-presentation-point-blank-reservoir-dogs> (accessed 3 October 2022).

99 Philip French, '*Point Blank* – Review', *Guardian*, 30 March 2013. Available at: <https://www.theguardian.com/film/2013/mar/31/point-blank-boorman-review-french> (accessed 29 September 2022).

100 'Director Jim Jarmusch Tests Limits in "Control"', *npr.org*, 8 May 2009. Available at: <https://www.npr.org/transcripts/103902528> (accessed 27 September 2022).

101 Lanie Goodman, 'Refn Revs into High Gear with "Drive"', *Wall Street Journal*, 4 November 2011. Available at: <https://www.wsj.com/articles/SB10001424052970203554104577003312845375528> (accessed 15 September 2022).

Credits

Point Blank
USA
1967

Directed by
John Boorman
Produced by
Judd Bernard
Robert Chartoff
Screenplay by
Alexander Jacobs
David Newhouse
Rafe Newhouse
based on the novel *The Hunter* by Richard Stark
Director of Photography
Philip H. Lathrop

©1967 Metro-Goldwyn-Mayer, Inc.
Metro-Goldwyn-Mayer presents
A Judd Bernard–Irwin Winkler Production

Assistant Director
Al Jennings
Music
Johnny Mandel
Edited by
Henry Berman
Art Direction
Albert Brenner
George W. Davis
Set Decoration
F. Keough Gleason
(as Keough Gleason)
Henry Grace
Makeup
William Tuttle

Hairstyling
Sydney Guilaroff
Unit Production Manager
Edward Woehler
Recording Supervisor
Franklin Milton
Special Visual Effects
J. McMillan Johnson
Colour Consultant
William Stair
Production Associate
Patricia Casey
Assistant to Producer
Rafe Newhouse
Production Photographs
David Steen
Dialogue Coach
Norman Stuart

uncredited
Producer
Irwin Winkler
Assistant Directors
Mickey Lewis
Christopher Seitz
Costume Design
Margo Weintz
Makeup
John Truwe
Leadman
Matty Azzarone
Painter
Frank Wesselhof
Boom
Clint Althouse
Sound Recordist
Frank Antunez
Sound Editor
Van Allen James

Sound Mixer
Larry Jost
Stunts
Boyd Cabeen
Jerry Catron
Bill Hickman
Chuck Hicks
Carey Loftin
Ted White
Still Photographer
Virgil Apger
Assistant Camera
William N. Clark
Camera Operator
Cliff King
Wardrobe
Lambert Marks
Margo Weintz
Location Manager
Robert Sunderland
Musicians
Robert Armbruster
Paul Beaver
Harry Bluestone
Ray Brown
Billy Byers
George 'Red' Callender
Gene Cipriano
Victor Feldman
Artie Kane
Mel Lewis
Virginia Majewski
Johnny Mandel
Red Mitchell
Uan Rasey
Emil Richards
Aaron Rochin
Bud Shank
Ray Sherman
Script Supervisor
Doris Grau

CAST
Lee Marvin
Walker
Angie Dickinson
Chris
Keenan Wynn
Yost
Carroll O'Connor
Brewster
Lloyd Bochner
Frederick Carter
Michael Strong
Stegman
John Vernon
Mal Reese
Sharon Acker
Lynne
James Sikking
hired gun
Sandra Warner
waitress
Roberta Haynes
Mrs Carter
Kathleen Freeman
first citizen

Victor Creatore
Carter's man
Lawrence Hauben
car salesman
Susan Holloway
girl customer
Sid Haig
1st penthouse lobby
guard
Michael Bell
2nd penthouse lobby
guard
Priscilla Boyd
receptionist
John McMurtry
messenger
Ron Walters
George Strattan
young men in apartment
Nicole Rogell
Carter's secretary
Rico Cattani
Roland La Starza
(as Roland LaStarza)
Reese's guards

Production Details
Filmed 20 February –
27 April 1967 on
location in Los Angeles,
California, USA; Alcatraz
Island, California, USA;
San Francisco, California,
USA
35mm
2.35:1
Colour (Metrocolor)
MPAA no.: 21489
Running time:
92 minutes

Release Details
Premiered in San
Francisco on 30 August
1967. US theatrical
release on 31 August
1967 by MGM

Bibliography

Bates, Dan, 'Review of *Point Blank* by John Boorman', *Film Quarterly* 21:2 (Winter 1967–8), p. 63.

Boorman, John, *Adventures of a Suburban Boy* (London: Faber and Faber, 2003).

_____, Interviewed by Michel Ciment, *John Boorman*, trans. Gilbert Adair (London: Faber and Faber, 1986), p. 76.

_____, 'My Difficult Friend', *Irish Times*, 13 June 1998. Available at: <https://www.irishtimes.com/news/my-difficult-friend-1.162944> (accessed 7 July 2022).

_____, 'Notes', Boorman, John MSS, 1940–2014, Subseries *Point Blank* (1967), LMC 2889, Lilly Library, Indiana University, Bloomington.

_____, *Point Blank*, DVD Commentary (Burbank, CA: Warner Home Video, 2014).

Bradshaw, Peter, '*Point Blank* – Review', *Guardian*, 29 March 2013. Available at: <https://www.theguardian.com/film/2013/mar/28/point-blank-review> (accessed 20 July 2022).

Brown, John Lindsay, 'Islands of the Mind', *Sight and Sound* 39:1 (Winter 1969–70), pp. 20–5.

Carringer, Robert, 'Hollywood's Los Angeles: Two Paradigms', *Looking for Los Angeles: Architecture, Film, Photography, and the Urban Landscape*, eds Charles D. Salas and Michael S. Roth (Los Angeles, CA: Getty Research Institute, 2001), pp. 247–66.

Cowie, Peter, '*Point Blank* to *Hiroshima Mon Amour*', in *Revolution! The Explosion of World Cinema in the 1960s* (London: Faber and Faber, 2004).

Crowther, Bosley, 'Vengeful Lee Marvin in "Point Blank"', *New York Times*, 19 September 1967.

Danks, Adrian, 'A Man Out of Time: John Boorman and Lee Marvin's *Point Blank*', *Senses of Cinema* 45, November 2007. Available at: <https://www.sensesofcinema.com/2007/cteq/point-blank/> (accessed 20 July 2022).

De Palma, Brian, 'Guilty Pleasures: Brian De Palma', *Film Comment* 23:3 (May–June 1987), pp. 52–3.

'Director Jim Jarmusch Tests Limits in "Control"', *npr.org*, 8 May 2009. Available at: <https://www.npr.org/transcripts/103902528> (accessed 27 September 2022).

Duffy, Michael S., 'Eurovisions: Alternative Views of the Hollywood Landscape', *World Film Locations: Los Angeles*, ed. Gabriel Solomons (Bristol: Intellect Books, 2011), pp. 122–3.

Ebert, Roger, 'Point Blank', *Chicago Sun-Times*, 20 October 1967.

Epstein, Dwayne, 'Exclusive: Frequent Costar Angie Dickinson on Lee Marvin', Dwayne Epstein: Author of *Lee Marvin: Point Blank*, 24 November 2014. Available at: <http://pointblankbook.com/exclusive-frequent-costar-angie-dickinson-on-lee-marvin/> (accessed 13 July 2022).

_____, 'Johnny Mandel: Point Blank's Composer', Dwayne Epstein: Author of *Lee Marvin: Point Blank*, 5 July 2020. Available at: <http://pointblankbook.com/johnny-mandel-point-blanks-composer/> (accessed 14 July 2022).

_____, *Lee Marvin: Point Blank* (Tucson, AZ: Schaffner Press, 2013).

Farber, Manny, 'The Train, Bonnie and Clyde, Reflections in a Golden Eye, Point Blank', *Artforum* 6:4 (December 1967), pp. 68–9.

Farber, Stephen, 'The Outlaws', *Sight and Sound* 37:4 (Autumn 1968), pp. 174–5.

French, Philip, 'Point Blank – Review', *Guardian*, 30 March 2013. Available at: <https://www.theguardian.com/film/2013/mar/31/point-blank-boorman-review-french> (accessed 29 September 2022).

Goodman, Lanie, 'Refn Revs into High Gear with "Drive"', *Wall Street Journal*, 4 November 2011. Available at: <https://www.wsj.com/articles/SB10001424052970203554104577003312845375528> (accessed 15 September 2022).

Hampton, Howard, 'Face Off: Howard Hampton on Red River and Point Blank', *Artforum*, 18 July 2014. Available at: <https://www.artforum.com/film/howard-hampton-on-red-river-and-point-blank-47418> (accessed 13 July 2022).

Harris, Mark, 'Cinema '67 Revisited: Point Blank', *Film Comment*, 30 August 2017. Available at: <https://www.filmcomment.com/blog/cinema-67-revisited-point-blank/> (accessed 18 July 2022).

Hill, Walter, Interviewed by Patrick McGilligan, *Backstory 4: Interviews with Screenwriters of the 1970s and 1980s*, ed. Patrick McGilligan (Berkeley: University of California Press, 2006).

Hirsch, Foster, *Detours and Lost Highways: A Map of Neo-Noir* (New York: Limelight, 1999).

Hoyle, Brian, *The Cinema of John Boorman* (Lanham, MD: Scarecrow Press, 2012).

Jacobs, Alexander, Interviewed by Stephen Farber, 'The Writer II: An Interview with Alexander Jacobs', *Film Quarterly* 22:2 (Winter 1968–9), pp. 2–14.

_____, Letter of 19 December 1966, Boorman, 'Correspondence, 1966–1969', in Boorman, John MSS, 1940–2014, Subseries *Point Blank* (1967), LMC 2889, Lilly Library, Indiana University, Bloomington.

_____, Letter of 20 March 1967, Boorman, 'Correspondence, 1966–1969', in Boorman, John MSS, 1940–2014, Subseries *Point Blank* (1967), LMC 2889, Lilly Library, Indiana University, Bloomington.

_____, David Newhouse and Rafe Newhouse, 'Point Blank: Original Story, Based on the Novel The Hunter, by Richard Stark', Film Script, 14 August 1967, BFI Collections, Reuben Library, SCR 14306, Reel 2.

Kael, Pauline, *5001 Nights at the Movies* (New York: Picador, 1991).

Lesner, Sam, 'Lee Marvin's Violent World', *Washington Post*, 15 October 1967.

Lewis, Peter, 'Is "Point Blank" a Ghost Story?', *Medium*, 21 October 2012. Available at: <https://medium.com/@plewis67/is-point-blank-a-ghost-story-c81174dc86c5> (accessed 14 July 2022).

Lines, Alex, 'Point Blank: Dissecting a
    Forgotten Classic', Film Inquiry,
    1 August 2016. Available at: <https://
    www.filminquiry.com/point-blank-
    retrospective/> (accessed 14 July
    2022).

Martin, James Michael, 'Point Blank by
    John Boorman, Judd Bernard',
    Film Quarterly 21:4 (Summer 1968),
    pp. 40–3.

Morreale, Jeanne, 'Dreams and
    Disruption in the Fifties Sitcom',
    E-Media Studies 4:1, 2015. Available
    at: <https://journals.dartmouth.
    edu/cgi-bin/WebObjects/Journals.
    woa/xmlpage/4/article/453>
    (accessed 7 October 2022).

Nicholson, Amy, 'Young Quentin
    Goes to the Movies: How "Point
    Blank" Influenced Tarantino's
    Directorial Debut "Reservoir Dogs"',
    The Ringer, 25 July 2019. Available
    at: <https://www.theringer.
    com/2019/7/25/20727062/quentin-
    tarantino-feature-presentation-
    point-blank-reservoir-dogs>
    (accessed 3 October 2022).

'North America (US and Canada)
    Domestic Movie Chart for 1967',
    The Numbers. Available at:
    <https://www.the-numbers.com/
    market/1967/top-grossing-movies>
    (accessed 21 July 2022).

Point Blank Pressbook (Hollywood, CA:
    M-G-M, 1967).

Press, Andrea, 'Gender and Family in
    Television's Golden Age and Beyond',
    The Annals of the American Academy
    of Political and Social Science 625,
    September 2009, pp. 139–50.

Schager, Nick, 'Review: Point Blank',
    Slant, 24 July 2003. Available at:
    <https://www.slantmagazine.com/
    film/point-blank/> (accessed 14 July
    2022).

Shadoian, Jack, Dreams and Dead Ends:
    The American Gangster/Crime Film
    (Cambridge, MA: MIT Press, 1977).

Shklovsky, Viktor, 'Art as Technique',
    Modern Criticism and Theory: A Reader,
    ed. David Lodge (London: Longmans,
    1988), pp. 16–30.

Solomons, Gabriel, 'Los Angeles',
    Big Picture Magazine 16 (September/
    October 2011), p. 26.

Spicer, Andrew, 'Problems of Memory
    and Identity in Neo-Noir's
    Existential Anti-Hero', The Philosophy
    of Neo-Noir, ed. Mark T. Conrad
    (Lexington: University of Kentucky
    Press, 2007).

Thomas, Kevin, 'Chartoff and Winkler:
    Entrepreneurs of the Offbeat Film
    Two Entrepreneurs of Offbeat
    Movies', Los Angeles Times,
    16 January 1968.

Thomson, David, 'A Very Bad Man', Sight
    and Sound 23:4 (April 2013), pp. 36–40.

____, 'As I Lay Dying', Sight and Sound
    8:6 (June 1998), pp. 14–17

____, 'Mission Intractable', Sight and
    Sound 16:2 (February 2006), pp. 28–30.

____, The New Biographical Dictionary of
    Film: Sixth Edition (New York: Knopf,
    2014).

Wasserman, John L., 'Point Blank', San
    Francisco Chronicle, 15 October 1967.

Winkler, Irwin, Life in the Movies:
    Stories from Fifty Years in Hollywood
    (New York: Abrams, 2019).